Managing from the Heart

A Way of Life

The Manager's

Tool Box

Managerial tools for developing self and staff

by

Larry D. Braley

&

Ray D. Gragg

At Manager Development Services, we do one thing and one thing only; we specialize in training managers in the "art" of managing people.

For full line of our training products: e-learning courses, books, workbooks, workshops, training, and consulting services, visit

www.managerdevelopment.net

ISBN: 978-0-557-02701-9

Managing from the Heart

❧ The Manager's Tool Box ❧

This book is designed to be a "quick reference" guide to using tools that will enhance the quality and productivity of any person's life.

It is important to understand that tools cannot build or repair anything. It's only the person who is willing to pick them up and use them that can build or repair something. It's also important to understand that practice makes better. It doesn't make perfect; it makes better. The more often you use a particular tool, the more natural and adept you become at using it.

What is a tool? Simply, a tool is a technique, exercise, method, ritual, or trick – any thing – you can use which will help you change or enhance a behavior. This is a more defined list of tools mentioned in the book, "Managing from the Heart." Some are explained here and some are explained more detail within the text itself and you will be referred to the chapter or page number.

Some tools are used to change unhealthy behaviors, some are used for attitude adjustments, some for effective interaction with people, some for emotional growth, some for spiritual growth, and some for living in reality.

For our purposes, our list of tools has been broken down into three main categories:

Tools for Developing as a Human Being

Tools for Developing as a Manager

Tools for Developing Staff

For a full understanding of a particular tool (when and how to use it, what to look for, or how to interpret the outcome) you may want to reference the text itself.

1

The Manager's Tool Box

❧ Table of Contents ❧

Table of Contents

Tools for Developing as a Manager

Table of Contents

Tools for Developing Staff

Tools for Developing as a Human Being

These tools are used primarily for personal growth. As manager, you will want to impart some of these tools to members of your staff to use when you see them struggling with personal issues or suffering from self-destructive behaviors.

Growth doesn't stop unless you stop pursuing it.

1) What drives my life? (chapter #6)

What is my motivation in life? Is it money? ...power? ...love? ...fame? ...approval? Now consider what your life would be like if you had as much as you wanted. Would it be enough? Would you then be happy?

This is basically a "reality check" on what I am devoting my life too. We often set our sights on one thing when we actually desire something quite different. Eventually, we achieve what we think we wanted but feel empty.

It's a wise individual who knows what they want, works toward it, but remains grateful for what they have. Happiness comes from within – not without.

2) Gratitude List - What Is Here To Celebrate?

Write a list of fifty things you are grateful for today and put it in a safe place. Tomorrow, take out your list and read it out loud. Carry a pad of paper or a notebook with you throughout the day and jot down fifty more things you are grateful for today as you think of or notice them. Do this each day for four months: read your previous day's list and then write a new list. I will be surprised if you will want to stop at the end of four months. You will learn that the miracle isn't in the lists – it's in the learning to look for the beauty and blessings.

(example):   **Today, I am Grateful for:**

1. my grandson's laughter
2. cool, crisp, clean sheets at the end of a long, hard day
3. the murmuring of my daughter asleep on my chest
4. the smell of honeysuckle and the sound of crickets on a warm summer's night
5. the excitement in my son's eyes when he catches a fish
6. the awe of holding my wet baby for the first time
7. the first time I fell hopelessly in love
8. my grandfather's stories
9. the shy, awkward way my son kisses me goodnight
10. etc., etc., etc.

    (You only have to look for blessings to find them.)

3) Don't Fear Change – Embrace It!

If you want to change your life, I mean really change it, become willing to change everything.

We are naturally creatures of habit. We often become stuck in ruts and routines that "suck" the spontaneity and adventure out of life. Trudging through day-to-day life, we become bored and discontent. The regular becomes routine, the routine becomes a rut, the rut becomes a habit, and the habit becomes mundane and mechanical. Our lives become mundane and mechanical. Our lives loose meaning.

Have you ever pulled into your driveway and not remembered the drive home? Our behaviors become automatic – no thought or attention paid to them. Where were you during that period of the drive home?...LaLa Land? ...Zoned out? Were you living or merely existing?

Tools for Developing as a Human Being

If we keep on doing what we've always done – we will keep on getting what we've always gotten. If you're happy and content with what you've always gotten, then don't change a thing. But if you're not, then make the effort to change everything. Change the way you get up in the morning, what you have for breakfast, the route you drive to work, the greeting you give people, your desk or office, the place you have lunch, what you have to eat, your route home, where you shop, how you would eat dinner (turn off the TV, light candles, play music, sit down and talk with your spouse or children), your evening activity, what time you go to bed, the time the alarm is set. Change every little thing you can think of.

This will be extremely difficult at first and you will find yourself doing the "old rut stuff" without even realizing it. Change is uncomfortable – it feels unnatural and stressful and it's scary. That's ok – it takes time to change a behavior – it's a process.

Each day, when you get dressed, **put your watch on the opposite wrist it was on the day before.** This is a good reminder throughout your day to pay attention to things you can change. Imagine what life might be like if everything were new and different.

There's an old saying, "People will only change when it becomes too painful **not** too." But what if we loose fear of change and learn to embrace it? What if we were able to go through life not knowing and not fearing what to expect next? What if change became comfortable and we were able to accept life as it happens? Life becomes and adventure that gets to be lived instead of a task which has to be gotten through.

Life becomes interesting – you become interesting – you will discover new people, new places, new interests, and a new appreciation of your life.

4) Know your triggers - and what to do.

We all have triggers (things which trigger certain memories, emotions, or behaviors within us). Some triggers are positive (a favorite song may trigger joy and love, reminding us of a romance we experienced when we first heard the song). Some triggers are negative (someone laughs at us for making a mistake and we instantly feel the shame of countless other experiences when we were humiliated or made the butt of some joke). The experiences may be old and have nothing to do with the current situation or the intentions of the person laughing – but the pain is real – the pain doesn't know the difference, it hurts all the same.

Different triggers cause various pain – shame, anger, fear, frustration, humiliation, lust, remorse, resentment, etc. By identifying our triggers and separating the current situation from all the past situations, we learn to deal with the feelings at hand.

EXERCISE: ON A SEPARATE PIECE OF PAPER, write six lists of things which "trigger" 1) Fear, 2) Shame, 3) Anger, 4) Sadness, 5) Loneliness, and 6) Humiliation in you. Now write what you will do if confronted with each one. Share it with a friend.

---

5) Remember the WARNINGS SIGNS – "H.A.L.T."
HUNGRY, ANGRY, LONELY, TIRED!

Our brain, like our body, needs fuel, relaxation, stimulation, and rest. Whenever we allow ourselves to become too hungry we deprive our brain of the nutrients it needs to function properly. Our thoughts become clouded and sluggish. We become irritable and impatient. .

Anger is a very strong emotion which gives us an illusion of power or control. Notice, I said *illusion*. It often also causes us to throw reason out the window regardless of the consequences.

Loneliness is also a dangerous place for us to be. Are we lonely because we isolate? Or do we isolate because we are lonely? It doesn't matter because each feed off one another becoming a self-perpetuating cycle. I'm don't want to be around anyone, which makes me lonely, and the lonelier I feel the less I want to be around anyone. When I am lonely, I spend far too much time in the most dangerous place in the world for me – my own head – with my own thoughts – my own fears, self-pity, despair, insecurities, and vanity (self-pity is vanity disguised as suffering).

Feeling too tired or not getting enough rest also puts us in a dangerous place. Life becomes a chore and we begin to stop appreciating what we do have. We loose motivation to live and we begin just to exist. We become human doings instead of human beings.

When I'm hungry, I need to eat something healthy. When I'm angry, I need to call a close friend and talk it out. When I'm tired, I need to rest.

It doesn't matter if I want to or not. Whenever I am in any of these positions, I don't want to do anything that is good for me – and that's the point!

I don't have to want to do it – I just have to do it!

6) The phone is your friend and can save your life.

The phone can be a powerful friend and tool when used properly. We're fortunate in this day and age. With the prolific use of cell phones, support is at our fingertips 24/7. There's no reason a person cannot contact a friend or a loved one any time they need.

Once you have the names programmed, call someone. We need to not only learn but also practice new behaviors. Call at least three people each day even if it's just to say, "Hi." After awhile this new behavior will become second nature to you.

At first, you may find all kinds of reasons (excuses) why you shouldn't call – don't want to bother them, they're probably busy, they're probably eating dinner, etc. Recognize this as old behavior – old thinking. This is behavior and thinking we must change. This is your new program of change to enhance your life. Take care of yourself (it's ok) and do what you need to do to keep yourself healthy.

Consider this practice for the time when you really NEED to talk to someone. It's amazing how heavy the phone becomes and how vague the numbers seem and how powerful the reasons (excuses) sound at such times.

One thing you will discover is that people will love to hear from you even if it's only "Hi, how ya doing?"

Then, when the time comes that you NEED to talk, getting hold of someone will be easy – second nature for you.

7) Do something GOOD for someone else without them **or anyone** else knowing it was you that did it.

This is a gift to yourself really. Do something good for someone else without them **or anyone** else knowing it was you. Think – really think about what someone you know needs, then do or get it for them. The trick is: neither they nor anyone else can know it was you that did it. You will learn the value of giving selflessly without expecting anything in return.

Take a little time and figure out something really good you can do for someone else. Now I don't mean open a door or pull out a chair. Find something that someone really needs, something that could really help someone.

Now here's the catch – the tough part! No one, especially the person you do it for, can know that it was you that did it!

The first time I was given this as an assignment I responded with, "Wait a minute! Why do it if no one knows it's me?"

My mentor then explained if I have to let anyone know that it was I that did it then I'm not really doing it for someone else, I'm doing it for myself.

"But how are they going to know what a giving, selfless guy I am – how compassionate and caring I am?"

My mentor just shook his head (he shakes his head a lot). "That's my point! By not letting anyone know, you will learn the joy of giving without expecting anything in return."

Why should I need recognition, validation, and approval for doing something good? **Self-centeredness.** This tool helps us get out of "self" and recognize the value of service.

In healing, we need to get out of self and connect to others and the world around us. It's a process. It takes work. But the reward is unimaginable – priceless. You will find that this tool is a precious gift you give yourself.

8) Do something good for yourself - YOU DESERVE IT!

Do something good for yourself – **You Have Permission!!!** You don't have to feel guilty!!!

I don't mean treat yourself to an ice cream sundae or a lobster dinner. Do something really good for yourself. Give yourself a little dignity, a little respect, a little compassion, a little love.

I'd kill the son-of-a-bitch that treated me the way I did – but I did. I wouldn't let anyone hurt or abuse someone I cared deeply for so why would I allow someone hurt or abuse me? I can feel compassion today for someone who is hurting – who needs help. So why can't I have a little compassion for myself.

It's time to be on your own side. Choose to value yourself, treat yourself with respect, to stand up for your right to exist.

Be loving to yourself because you ARE loveable. You may not see it, but treat yourself lovingly and you will grow to see it.

Become willing to experience--to make real to yourself, without denial or evasion--that you think what you think, feel what you feel, desire what you desire, have done what you have done, and are what you are.

Have compassion for yourself. Be a friend to yourself. Your wants and dreams, your values and beliefs, your thoughts, opinions, and your feelings ARE important. No more important than anyone else's – but no less important either.

You are not perfect – and guess what – it's OK. No one else is perfect either. We are all perfectly imperfect. By working a program we discover our flaws but also those wonderful things about ourselves. In working a program, we learn to nurture the wonderful things and work on our flaws.
Remember – Progress Not Perfection.

9) Eat a balanced diet, exercise, & get plenty of sleep -- "**feeling**" healthy is a large part of "**being**" healthy.

Eat a balanced diet, exercise, and get plenty of sleep. Sounds simple doesn't it? Then why is it we have such a difficult time doing it?

We all have great intentions of one day starting that diet or exercise program but somehow we never get around to it

Embracing change filters to all areas of our lives. Getting ourselves healthy and keeping ourselves healthy is extremely important. When we feel slow, sluggish, and weak we loose motivation and desire. When we lose motivation and desire we become complacent and life becomes a chore.

Some of us have done extensive damage to our bodies and they are in need of constant monitoring and daily care. Others of us find that we are just very run down and out of shape. Whichever the case, we need to learn to love, care for, and respect ourselves – and that includes our bodies.

Bodies need fuel in order to operate properly. If we deprive them of proper nutrients they will draw these nutrients initially from fat. But fat is a poor source of nutrients so the body will begin to draw needed nutrients from muscle and organs. The more our body does, the harder it works, the more nutrients it requires. Exercise without eating properly significantly damages the body.

Muscles need nutrients and exercise to tone and grow. They also need rest to heal. Exercising a muscle actually tears it. Proper rest and nutrients allows muscle to repair itself stronger than it was before the exercise.

A body that is run down is prone to circulatory, skeletal, and neurological problems as well as long list of diseases and organ problems. Simple attention to the fuel we ingest, rest, exercise, and care we give our bodies is a sound way to insure physical well-being.

Feeling healthy – feeling alive – initiates a positive outlook on the world around us and gives us strength to deal with problems and change. It allows us to handle the stress of life's problems. When our physical self isn't healthy our emotional, mental, and spiritual selves aren't healthy either.

10) Learn to laugh from the gut, weep from the heart, and wonder in awe at the miracles all around you.

True freedom is the ability to be real, open, honest, and genuine. To feel secure within oneself allows a person to experience others and the world to its fullest. The old saying, "Laughter is the best medicine," is true. Laughter heals the heart.

The ability to weep from the heart is the ability to feel from the soul. Sadly, many people are emotionally dead, hardened, cut-off from the world around them. Most have been hurt so they build walls to keep out further pain. And the walls work. They do keep out further pain, but they also keep out the good as well. Walls keep out everything, but mostly, they keep out intimacy. Maybe that's why so many people feel so alone today.

Without the ability to weep, there is no intimacy. Without intimacy, there is no connectedness with people. Without connectedness, there is no joy and laughter, and without joy and laughter, one cannot wonder in awe at the miracles around them.

11) Become a student of life

Read a book you normally wouldn't, take a class, attend a workshop or seminar, etc. There is more in this world than anyone could ever comprehend. The more I learn, the more I weep at my ignorance. Enrich your life with knowledge and it becomes an adventure.

"There are more things in this world than are dreamt of in your philosophy"
William Shakespeare

12) Discover Your Passion

What do really love doing? What gives your life meaning?
Is it painting? playing music? building things? fishing?
dancing? learning?

EXERCISE:

List 20 things you have never tried before and resolve to do
at least one of those things each week. You just may discover
something wonderful. If you find you really don't like
something, well, you don't have to do it ever again. But at least
you'll know. Having trouble coming up with 20 things? What
does that tell you?

---

13) Stay off the "pity pot" - take a friend and volunteer at a
shelter for the homeless or abused children.

"Nobody likes me. Nobody understands me. I've caused so
much damage, hurt so many loved ones. I'm such a horrible
person. Life is so hard. I'll never be able to make it up to
everyone. No one hurts as much as I. No one has been
mistreated as badly as I. No one has been betrayed as much as I.
No one suffers like I. Woe is me."

Well, you're absolutely right. Woe is you – for acting this
way. Get off the cross, we need the wood. Remember, self-pity
is actually vanity disguised as suffering. And yes, you may have
pain. You may have suffered. You may have been betrayed or
abused. But why do you so zealously hold onto this pain. Yes,
life is hard – as hard as you make it. You can be the best person
you can be today. But as long as you wallow in that pain,
refusing to let it go, you will continue to suffer.

What do you want to do? Just lay down and die? Or do you
want to live – to make a difference?

It's often hard to recognize when we're feeling sorry for
ourselves. It's also hard to do anything about it because self-pity,
like boredom kills motivation. We become very comfortable

18

wallowing in our misery and very often come to wear it like a badge of honor.

What Arrogance!!!

Once again, we need to get out of "self" and the best way to do this is to be of service. Call a close friend and volunteer at a homeless shelter, a home for abused children, a home for the elderly, etc. Anywhere you can help someone less fortunate than yourself – and don't make any excuses, there's always someone less fortunate than you.

Believe me, when a child gives you a sincere, heartfelt, "Thank you," for plopping a ladle full of goop on a metal tray your perspective and appreciation of your world changes.

14) A Pocket full of Dimes.

In changing a behavior, it is necessary to be constant until a healthy behavior becomes natural (and replaces) the unhealthy behavior. A woman told her husband that she loves to be hugged. He came from a family that was not affectionate and didn't like hugging. He loved her and wanted to please her so he decided to start hugging her. He put 10 dimes in his right pocket. Throughout the day, every time he hugged her he would take a dime out of his right pocket and put it in his left. At the end of the day, he would count the dimes in his left pocket to see how well he did.

15) What Do I Want For My Life?   (chap 7)

Is this how you envisioned your life? Are you happy? ...content? What would you like to see different? I can't count the number of clients I've worked with over the years who weren't living their own lives. I've had clients who became lawyers because Dad was a lawyer and Dad's dad was a lawyer when all they really wanted to do was paint. I've had clients who became doctors because "we've always had doctors in the family" when all they really wanted to do was build things or dance or teach. They were so busy living someone else's life they didn't have a chance to live their own.

19

The Manager's Tool Box

What happens to a codependent when they die? Somebody else's life flashes before their eyes. Imagine: you're old and gray, lying on your deathbed, looking back over your life and you realize that you never went on that trip you always dreamed of, you never rode those rapids you always talked about, or never shared that special time with your kids that you meant to because you were always too busy. After all, there would always be another day, wouldn't there? Another day, another vacation, another opportunity to do everything – "and man what fun we'll have then." But somehow, it never happened. Somehow, life got in the way.

And then you realize, that your finite time on this earth, your one and only life -- is spent.

We get so busy with life we don't spend any time living it. We become human doings instead of human beings. And then we make that fatal mistake...we blink and it's over.

If you had it to do over again, what would you do differently? How would want to spend it? Well, instead of looking back 20 or 30 years from now regretting -- thinking about what you should have done differently today – DO IT TODAY!!!! Don't spend the next 20 or 30 years building regrets. Don't waste your life.

Ask yourself, "What do I want out of my one and only life?" This life is yours – let others live theirs.

EXERCISE: Write 4 lists describing, "What do I want my life to be like
      1) one year from now?"
      2) five years from now?"
      3) 10 yrs.?"
      4) 20 yrs.?"

Now, write how you see the things and people in your life at each of these times.
Where do you want to be physically, emotionally, spiritually?
What do you want to look back on with gratitude and contentment?

What regrets do you **not** want to have?

16) Take your own daily inventory - NOT OTHER'S!

It's too easy to recognize and point out flaws in others, but when I find myself doing this I must ask myself, "Why?" I usually find that I'm doing it to avoid looking at myself. What is it that is going on in me that makes me judgmental toward someone I don't even know?

Instead of looking at others, I should be concerned about how I am doing. Am I doing the right things? Do I want to be a person who looks for the flaws in others or do I want to be a person that looks for the goodness in others. Personally, I try to be the best person I can be each and every day. Each morning when I wake up, I make this a conscious decision. Throughout my day I try to aware of anytime I offend or hurt someone, and when I do, I do my best to set it right, right then. I don't want to wait till late. Remember the bricks? I don't want to carry any bricks any longer than I have too.

In the evening before bed, I look back over my day and if I can honestly say I haven't hurt anyone, not even me, then I've had a great day.

17) Pursuit of Humility - if you "think" you are humble, you're not. Your **reward** is in the **pursuit** of humility.

The principle of humility states that all human beings are equal—nobody is better or worse than another. It means having respect for the inner dignity of every person—to speak to that part of them that is their beauty and goodness instead of their ugliness and badness. Look for that part of God in everyone.

The pursuit of humility keeps us grounded in reality and instills in us a sense of compassion both for ourselves and others. It's the pursuit of humility which keeps us from becoming **self-righteous**.

What arrogance! -- What ignorance! -- What innocence!

18) Street Cleaning - keep your side of the street clean.

This tool is used in conjunction with "tool #16." Perform Reality Checks (tool #51) throughout your day, be honest, and ask yourself if you have hurt or mistreated anyone. If you answer, "Yes," now is the time to go and set right your part of whatever happened. We can't control anyone else. All we can do is make sure we've cleaned up anything we are responsible for.

EXERCISE: Think of a time you got into an argument with someone and you said or even did things you normally wouldn't do – you would normally find unacceptable.

1. Ask yourself, "Did I say or do things I find inappropriate or shameful?" Now be honest with yourself. Your first inclination will be to justify your actions because the other individual said or did this or that. What the other individual has done has nothing to do with it – it doesn't matter what they did. Their baggage is their baggage – let them carry it.

2. Ask yourself, "Why did I give this other person the power to make me say and do things I am not proud of?"

3. Ask yourself, "What might I have said or done differently?"

4. Ask yourself, "Do I regret having said or done those things?" If your answer is no, then ask yourself, "Why am I unwilling to let go of the feelings surrounding this incident?" "Am I still angry?" "Am I still justifying my behavior?"

5. If you are willing to give up the pain (frustration, shame, resentment, hurt, etc.) then go to the individual and:
   a. validate what you said or did that you wish you hadn't,
   b. admit your behavior was inappropriate and you regret having done it,
   c. apologize for YOUR behavior (do not explain why you did it),
   d. ask the individual how you can make it up to them.

Now here is the important thing, you are doing this to clean up YOUR side of the street. You are not attempting to clean up their side of the street and you are not looking for an apology from them. Do not expect them to understand or reciprocate. I guarantee if you do, you will be disappointed and will even develop a new resentment.

The idea is to acknowledge and let go of the pain you have created in your life. This sets you free. When you go to bed, you will be able to look back over your day and feel good about you.

19) Beating yourself up -- with a belt

No one can beat us up the way we can. We are our own worst critics. By the time we are twenty years old, we have 35 thousand hours of "Self-talk" tape running through our heads – 80% of which is negative. Whether it's criticism from someone else or from ourselves, we cause the most pain in our lives. (see Tool #21)

Most of us find ourselves judging, chastising, or scolding ourselves for not living up to some unrealistic expectation we have of ourselves. Physical wounds will usually heal by themselves given time. Emotional and spiritual wounds fester – become worse with time. Why do we find it so difficult to hold a compliment in our heart for more than just a fleeting moment?

EXERCISE:
Whenever you realize you are "beating yourself up" with this negative "self-talk" – stop what you are doing, take off your belt, and begin to beat yourself on your back. Wherever you are, whatever you are doing – STOP and beat yourself. Continue this until you begin to realize how stupid and self-destructive it is – then STOP and ask yourself,
"Why am I doing to my soul what I'm doing to my back?" Then use Tool # 80.

20) Make a Balance Wheel - is your life balanced?

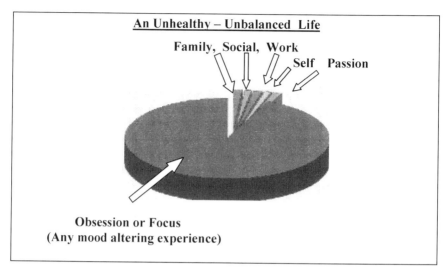

An Unhealthy – Unbalanced Life

Family, Social, Work

Self   Passion

Obsession or Focus
(Any mood altering experience)

All of us have special talents and can do amazing things; we just have trouble doing life. Without even being aware of it, we can find ourselves focused, even obsessed, on one area or another of our lives and do not realize that the other areas are suffering. In a sense, we become addicted to one area. Whenever we fail to have balance in our lives – whenever we allow one part to become so important that it edges out others, we will have consequences. If we allow it to continue long enough, we will have **life-damaging consequences.**

Example: Unfortunately in our culture, workaholics are often revered. Considered "movers and shakers" in the industry, self-made men, pulled himself up by his bootstraps; these people have become addicted to work. Like any addiction, it's the addiction itself which inhibits the individual from recognizing and admitting that there is really a problem. Yes, he may make a lot of money and accomplish great things and get great satisfaction from his efforts, but he will eventually loose his family, his purpose, and maybe even his life.

Having little or no time for his wife and children, they learn to live without him. They've learned they can't count on him to show up at their Little League game or their recital or family functions. In essence, they've lost him to work. The children may grow up angry and resentful or simply indifferent. Often, there is divorce and the family goes on to live their lives. Originally, he may have worked to have a life, but somewhere along the line the only thing that became important – the only thing which gives live any meaning is his work.

He may develop blood pressure problems, ulcers, heart problems, suffer from stress and anxiety, etc. In the end, when he is lying on his death bed, all he will have to comfort him are the memories of the "Big Deals" he pushed through as he is told that the office has already gotten someone to replace him.

Interestingly enough, most people become psychologically or behaviorally dependent (addicted) to something sometime in their lives. To change an addiction takes work – it's not easy.

Activity Addictions: any activity can be used to alter feelings through distraction (i.e.: work, shopping, sex, food, relationships, religious rituals, gambling, exercise, etc.).

Cognitive Addictions: living in your head to avoid feelings, over-analyzing, worrying, obsessing.

Feeling Addictions: rageaholic – rage covers up shame, pain, and helplessness giving one the *illusion* of power and control over a situation. Fear becomes an overwhelming sense of dread creating distrust, foreboding, and eventually paranoia. Sadness/grief becomes a badge of martyrdom and honor soliciting attention and sympathy. Joy is often used to avoid reality, hiding pain, to make people think you're o.k.

Thing Addictions: money, possessions, toys, collectables, relationships (people become objects and collectables), etc.

By getting honest with ourselves and becoming willing to change our lives is the first step. We need to remain aware on a daily basis about whether we are obsessing on any one thing. We must make an effort to keep all areas of our lives in balance, understanding that any area which isn't nurtured will suffer and eventually die.

A Healthy Balanced Life

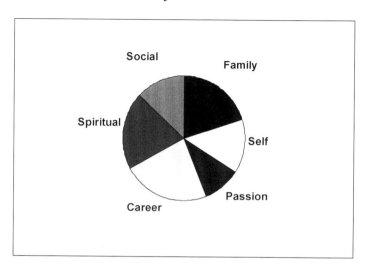

Self: health (physical, mental, emotional, psychological)

Work: work to live – not live to work

Family: immediate and extended need not only your time but attention as well

Spiritual: pray, meditate, give service or whatever you need to do to connect to yourself and that to which we are all a part of

Social Life: friends and acquaintances enrich your life

Passion: that which fills your heart with aliveness, purpose, meaning – whether it's to paint, dance, sing, write, create, build things, etc.

By keeping our lives in balance, we nurture everything which gives our existence meaning. We become fulfilled and whole.

Tools for Developing as a Human Being

21) Mirror Work – positive affirmations!

Mirror work is one of most powerful tools to change negative the self-talk that keeps us in a cycle of repeating self-defeating behaviors. To change this destructive self-talk, you need to change the "core belief" that drives it. This self-talk becomes a self-fulfilling prophecy. These "core beliefs" are false.

EXERCISE:
Stand in front of the mirror for five minutes in the morning and five minutes in the evening. Study the person you see looking back at you – the eyes, hair, mouth, jaw line, smile, frown, lips, etc. Talk to this person. Get to know this person. This is your next "best friend" – a friend who will never leave you. Say positive affirmations to this person out loud.

Affirmations

Today, I begin a new Life.

I rejoice in being alive. I am getting to know myself and learning to love myself.

I am not perfect and that is a good thing. I no longer have to try to be perfect.

I give myself permission to be human.

My opinions are as valid and as important as anyone's.

I am loveable just because I am unique—there is no one else like me.

I do not have to prove myself to anyone. I am whole and good. I am precious.

I am smart, warm, and capable. I am beautiful inside and outside.

I can meet my own needs.

I deserve love, peace, prosperity and serenity.

I can set my own boundaries.

I cannot be abused unless I allow it. And today I will allow it no longer.

I forgive myself for hurting myself and for letting others hurt me.

I forgive myself for nurturing myself and others.

Guilt and blame are luxuries I can do without.

Just for today, I will respect my own and other's boundaries.

Just for today, I will be open and honest with someone I trust.

Just for today, I will take one compliment and hold it in my heart for more than just a fleeting moment. I will let it nurture me.

I let go of my expectations of others. They are free to be themselves and I am free to be me.

I am intelligent and sensitive. I am willing to receive love. I love myself unconditionally.

I am loved because I deserve love. I am not alone. I am enough. I reclaim power over my life.

As you say these affirmations, you will feel silly and you will not believe a word. That's ok! You can't change a lifetime of negative self-talk overnight. You will not believe it, but you will be on your way to believing it. And that's what matters.

22) Play the tape ALL the way through.

When faced with a temptation to do something that you know is not healthy for you, stop and imagine that you are in a movie. Now play this movie in your mind. Imagine yourself doing what is tempting you. Imagine how much you will enjoy it. But don't stop here! Now continue playing the tape. Imagine what it will be like later, after the "fun" part is over. Imagine what you will feel like. Are you happy? Or maybe you feel guilty? Are others involved? Are they affected? Is anyone hurt?

When tempted, we often fanaticize and idealize the temptation but don't even think about the consequences. We romance the pleasure but discount the pain. Afterward, we're often filled with regret. Sometimes we hurt others or ourselves and then beat ourselves up for being so mean or stupid. When we realize the consequences of our actions and weigh the potential pleasure against the potential pain, we are better able to make healthy, disciplined choices.

23) Today is Life

The Past is only a memory, the Future just a wish. It's amazing how many people are living in the past or the future while missing the present. Many obsess on past regrets – what should have beens, if onlys, why didn't Is.

Some people continually romance the past, longing for a time they remember – a time they have idealized in their minds, making it much better than it really was. The ironic thing is that these times they long for, these times that were so perfect, were probably missed when they were being lived because the individual was obsessing on another, even previous, past.

People who live in regrets continually beat themselves up for nothing that can be changed. No one can change the past. All of us would like to go back and change something, but we can't. What we can do though is change today. We can do something about today, something that can prevent us from someday looking back at today with regret.

Others live in the future. When that "Big Deal" goes through, when I win the lotto, when this or that happens, when that one "perfect" person comes into our life, then we will be happy, then we will start living. Sadly, tomorrow is not promised to anyone, young and old alike. Graveyards are full of people still waiting.

The only time any of us really have is now. Life is now. It's ok to remember the past, but not to live in the past. It's ok to plan for the future, but not to live in the future. If you're living in the past or you're living in the future – you're not living.

If you really want to live, then celebrate what there is in each and every moment for this moment will NEVER come again and we only get so many moments.

24) "Good-bye Letters"

If you have ever experienced a relationship in your life (and we all have), then you will also have experienced pain. If you grieve over the loss of someone or someone has deeply wounded you, write them a letter expressing both the pain and the joy you've experienced in knowing them. Pour out your soul and do not hold anything back.

When you are finished, find some place special to you where you can be alone and read the letter out loud as if you are reading it to them – it doesn't matter that they can't hear it – you're doing this for you, not them. Then burn the letter and let its smoke melt in the wind to be carried to every living thing.

Nearly everyone has some sort of open wound they carry around with them. These wounds need closure. We need to heal and this tool is a step in the process.

25) Baby Steps - no one ever climbed a mountain in one big step.

In this text, we mention how, "stereotypically," women are plodders while men are sprinters. Women understand the power of "stone upon stone, percept upon precept." If I want to walk to Buenos Aires, the first thing I need to do is take one foot and place in front of the other. If I continue to do this, I will make it to Buenos Aires.

Often we see a task as overwhelming or insurmountable (let's admit it, Buenos Aires is one hell of a long walk). Because it seems overwhelming. Many will not even try and most will put it off as long as they possibly can. A few will actually throw a second pair of shoes in a bag and start.

26) Share your happiness with others.

The shortest distance between two people is a smile. Remember the orange? We attract what we project. Make it a practice to share a smile with at least five people each day. First of all, you will discover that when you smile YOU feel better.

Secondly, I guarantee you will be surprised at the reactions you will get. Kindness is infectious.

27) Change old routines and patterns.

Many of us find ourselves in a rut not knowing how we got there. Well, we try something and find it comfortable so every time we do that thing again, we begin to do it the same way we did when we found it comfortable or convenient. Eventually, it becomes a behavior and we just do it on autopilot. Have you ever driven home from work, pulled into your driveway, and not remembered the drive itself?

Because we do it on autopilot, it becomes rote and mundane. We no longer appreciate it as being comfortable or convenient. Instead, we begin to view it as uncomfortable, inconvenient, and a chore – but we keep doing it the same old way anyway.

Make a concerted effort to change everything in your life you can. Take a different route to work each day (yes, it may take longer, but you'll see different things). Wear you watch on your opposite wrist (this will really freak you out). Get out of bed at a different time each morning. Change what to have for breakfast, the clothes you usually wear, the coffee shop or Starbuck's where you usually stop (I'm not saying stop Starbuck's. I personally think that may be going a little too far).

This will be EXTREMELY uncomfortable at first, but soon you start to enjoy meeting new people, seeing new places, and trying new things.

28) What do I want to do? / What is the healthy thing to do?

As human beings, we are condemned to have to make choices. We make thousands of choices each day – some healthy and some unhealthy. All choices have consequences. The healthy choices have positive consequences and the unhealthy choices have negative consequences.

Why would anyone knowingly make an unhealthy choice and accept negative consequences? Well, often it's the unhealthy choices which seem the most enticing and we're usually very good at minimizing the consequences or lying to ourselves that they won't happen at all – that we won't have to face or deal with them. Then, when we're faced with dealing with them we beat ourselves up for making that choice.

Most of us are so good at lying to ourselves that we actually con ourselves into believing that an unhealthy choice is a healthy one. This is the power of denial.

Normally, when "what I want to do" is confronted with "what I should do" we look for ways to justify why "what I want to do" is good, or at least OK, for us. But deep down we know the truth.

Imagine what it might feel like to feel good about your choices – to not have any regrets about what you have done haunting you. To know that you have done the right and healthy thing and can feel good about **yourself.**

Aww, that's the secret – the pay off: to feel good about yourself.

EXERCISE:

When faced with a choice;

Ask yourself, "What do I **want** to do?"

Now ask yourself, "What is the healthy thing to do?"

Ask yourself, "Will what I want to do have any negative consequences?"

"How will accepting this choice make me feel in the long run?"

"Will I feel good about myself?"

If the answer to this last question is, "No," then ask, "Why would I be willing to do anything that would not make me feel good about myself?"

"Shouldn't I love myself more than that?"

Tools for Developing as a Human Being

29) Stay out of Harm's Way

Stay away from unhealthy people, places, and things. Whiners and losers will bring you down. Shaming, critical, nagging, negative, and judgmental people love to vomit their poison on others. It's almost impossible not to get infected when hanging around such individuals. The old saying, "Misery loves company," is old because it's true.

Also stay away from abusive, manipulative, and controlling people. Remember in chapter #9, "if I allow someone to abuse me, I am guilty of self-abuse?" It's your responsibility to nurture you.

If I'm standing on a chair, is it easier for me to pull you up or for you to pull me down? You can't change others; that's their job. All anyone can do is change themselves.

30) Praying for your enemies

Pray for the health, well-being, happiness, and success for your enemies. Ask that they may receive all the blessings you ask for yourself. Tough? – you bet. But praying daily for your enemies releases you from the bondage of anger, hatred, jealousy, resentment, and hurt which does nothing but eats us alive from the inside out.

31) Journaling

Journaling is probably the most therapeutic tool. Most of us have difficulty identifying what or why we're feeling a certain way. Feelings often cloud rational thought. We either don't know how or we're afraid to express what's going on inside us so we "stuff" it. The problem is when we stuff it, it festers.

Journaling allows us to get out, to express, what's bothering us with safety. A journal is yours and yours alone. It's to be read only by you and no one else. Usually daily, sit down alone and just write everything you're feeling, thinking, wishing, desiring, hoping, and wishing. Just start writing – anything. Soon, your pen will take on a life of its own. By the time you stop, you'll find that you've written pages. And when you read it back you'll be surprised to find all that was in you just waiting to get out. Later, whether a week, a month, or a year, you'll read it again and learn and understand from a whole new perspective. (Note: Do not use a computer. Write it out. If using a computer, wanting to edit and spell check will distract you.)

32) Respect Your Physical Well-being

Our physical well-being is just as important as our emotional, mental, and spiritual well-being. Last time I checked, we only get one body and we should take care of it. Get regular check-ups from your doctor, dentist, optometrist, therapist, psychiatrist, etc. Follow their recommendations to care for your physical well-being. You are worth taking care of.

33) Priority List

It's ironic how life often gets in the way of living. We become so focused on the busy things that need to be done that we loose sight of the real reason we are doing them. Yes, bills need to be paid, things need to be fixed around the house, and errands ran, but sometimes we get so busy doing life that we don't live.

It's too easy to assume that we will always have time to do those "special" things that makes life worth living. Then one day we wake up and wonder where the years went.

One major mistake most parents make is – **they blink!** The next thing they know they're walking one of the most precious people in the world down the aisle or sending them off to college and they realize that the chance to do all those things they had planned and wanted to do with them and for them is gone.

Often, once the children are on their own, there are two people left in the house staring at one another wondering, "Who are you?" This couple, at one time, fawned over one another,

Tools for Developing as a Human Being

were absorbed in one another, they had dreams and plans of the things they wanted to do, and if one hurt the other shared the pain. Now they're strangers, wondering how it got this way.

We often do not realize how precious something is until we loose it. Then we realize how we took it for granted and would give anything to get it back – to do it over.

It's difficult in life's bustle to stay focused on what is really important – what really gives your life meaning – what needs to be nurtured.

A) Write a list of at least three things that are most important to you in life today:

      (example)   **1)** my wife

                2) my children

                3) my health

B) Now write at least three things <u>you have done</u> this past week to nurture each item on your list:

(example)   **(Note: the <u>action</u> words in each list)**

1) my wife:

I **bought** her a special little present and left it where she would find it when I wasn't around.

I **surprised** her when she got home with a candlelight dinner.

I **called** her three different times just to **tell** her I was thinking of her.

2) my children:

I **took** them camping and **taught** them how build a campfire.

I **played** video games with them twice.

I **tucked** them in each night.

3) my health:

I **stuck** to (pretty much) my diet.

I **did** my push-ups and my running three days.

I **kept** my Dr's. appointment.

C) **Now write three things <u>you will do </u>this next week to nurture each item on your list:**
    (example)   (Note: the <u>action</u> words in each list)

1) my wife:

I **will purchase** tickets to the play she wants to see.

I **will buy** four cards, **write** my feelings for my wife, and **hide** them where she will find them at different times throughout the week

I will **call** her at least four times during the week just to **say** "I love you."

2) my children:

I will **tuck** them in each night.

I will **help** them with their homework.

I will **take** them to the zoo.

3) my health:

I will **get** my lab work done on Tuesday

I will **make** a stronger effort to adhere to my diet.

I will **continue** my exercise program three days a week.

Don't loose sight of what is really important

34) Who Am I? Living with Purpose.

In your journal, daily write down your thoughts, dreams, and wishes. Write at least one paragraph describing who you are today. Flip back through your journal to one week earlier and read the paragraph for that day and compare it with the paragraph you wrote today.

Discovering who you are is a process, a journey – ever changing, ever evolving.

Now write a paragraph on what you are going to do to be you on purpose today and compare it to a week earlier.

35) Celebrate Life. Ever hear "I'll believe it when I see it?"

Some things you have to believe before you can see them. If you believe it, then you'll see it. Throughout your day, stop and ask yourself, "what is there to celebrate in this moment."

Tools for Developing as a Manager

36) Observation Book ("In the Heat of the Battle" File)
Chap 19 (pg. 275)

Throughout our day, we notice things that need attending too or think of good ideas but forget them because we're too busy with whatever's at hand. This is a nine-dollar tool that'll make you a million bucks. Also called a "In the Heat of the Battle File," the Observation Book is simply a 3-ring binder with fifty or more numbered sections. Each section has a few blank pages in it. The fist page in the binder should be a blank "Table of Contents" page.

As I observe, watching and listening, I jot down anything and everything I see which needs attending too. First I check the "Table of Contents" and if there isn't a section for what I need to note – I add one. I then flip to that section and make a quick note on what I see, hear, or think. It seems that it's usually when I'm the busiest (hence: "In the Heat of the Battle") that I notice things that need attention but I don't have time at that moment.

This tool allows me to go back later, remember what I was thinking, and either attend to it myself or delegate what needs to be done to someone else.

By using the binder, I am able to quickly jot down what I see, promptly forget about it, and refocus on the task at hand. Later, when there's a "lull in the battle," I can return to my binder and attend to what needs attending. Some possible sections may include:

Employees
> Sales Staff
> Operations Staff
> Support Staff
> Needs & Wants

Red Flags

Attitudes
Processes
Equipment
Supplies
Kingdoms and Territories
Politics

Goals – What steps do I need to take to get there? What steps will the department need to take to get there?

Success Factors – What are the critical steps necessary for each goal to be achieved? What are the obligatory steps? And what are the compulsory steps?

Standards – Using success factors, what standards must be established to ensure effectivity? Standards will need to be defined for each area and position within the department.

Ergonomics – Layout of offices and workspace for best "flow" and efficiency (I don't put my office fax machine in forklift maintenance and I don't put my receptionist next to the back door)

Advertising / Marketing – If this is done through a separate department then I will need a liaison. Otherwise, this must be initiated with imaginative, yet realistic, vision.

Landscaping

Notice "Landscaping?" I use this example to demonstrate that the Observation Book is used for anything and everything. As I was entering the building one morning, I noticed that the shrubs in a particular area were dying and one of the cement steps was cracked. A quick note in my binder reminded me later that day to call maintenance to check the shrubs (possible sprinkler failure) and to repair the step (potential lawsuit). It only took a minute and a phone call to prevent dead, unsightly shrubs and injury to a customer or staff.

Time Management Tools

37) Ten minutes of planning saves a day of confusion. It's often difficult when you're really busy to stop and take a few minutes to just organize and plan what you're going to do. You may feel like if you take this ten or fifteen minutes out, you will get even further behind. In reality, if you don't stop and take the time, you will end up jumping back and forth from one thing to another, having to go back and redo things, and wasting much more time in the process.

Just organizing what needs to be done helps reduce needless repetition. Planning the most efficient way of carrying out what needs to be done ensures a greater probability of success. Organize in a way that makes sense to, and is easiest for, you. One person's planning book may be clumsy for another. Whether you use a planner, notepad, calendar, or email, organizing and planning saves time and sanity.

38) Prioritize tasks. Decide what tasks will produce the most results and are the most important, and then concentrate your efforts on them. Pay particular attention to "time sensitive" tasks and those with a deadline. Whether you make a list, use numbers, or colors, follow in sequence to avoid jumping back and forth. One tendency is to take care of the quickest or easiest tasks first. This only prolongs the important and the necessary until they become overwhelming.

39) Deal with the urgent. The urgent often become emergencies when left unattended. Get them out of the way so they're not "hovering over your head."

40) Delegate. Don't bog yourself down with menial, time-consuming tasks, which could easily be done by someone who has the time.

41) Goals give direction. Goals allow you to stay focused on your objective. They help you stay on track and identify wastefulness. Remember, a viable goal must be desirable, realistic, perceptible, precise, and measurable.

42) Perpetual "To Do" list. This is basically a priority list in which tasks are crossed off, others moved to the top, and still others added in order of urgency or importance. This list becomes a living, breathing tool.

43) Don't obsess on perfection. Each task must be done right and be effective. But no task can be done perfectly. Don't waste time obsessing over a task that is already right and effective. A perfectionist can waste all day tweaking something that is already good while other tasks suffer.

44) Don't bite off more than you can chew. When faced with a large project or task, don't attempt to accomplish it all at once. Steady is much more effective than fast. Do a little each day. Chip away at it methodically and even the overwhelming becomes doable.

45) Beware of procrastination. It's all too easy when faced with what may seem like an overwhelming task to want to put it off for the present. Thoughts like; not having enough time to complete it now, I'll just get these few other things out of the way first, and I'm tired now, I need to wait until I'm fresher will get a task put off over and over again until I really don't have the time to finish it.

46) Figure in time interruptions and distractions. Understand that there will be interruptions. Allow a certain amount of time for interruptions and distractions as well as a block of time for priorities. Realize that the world made need you, but it won't stop if it doesn't get you. If possible, set periods during the day when you are not allowed to be disturbed unless the building is falling or on fire. I personally call this my "priority block." People will get use to coming to you either before or after this priority block of time.

47) "No!" is a complete sentence. It's alright to say, "No!" to the unimportant. We have a right to say no and not have to justify it to anyone. Be willing to tell others "no" during the block of time when you're not allowed to be disturbed. Don't worry; they'll be back if it's really important.

48) Utilize your best time of day. Some of us are morning people and some are afternoon or night people. If it takes me till mid-morning to really get cooking, then I will want to set my "priority block" of time during this period when I am at my best.

49) Give yourself a little credit. Don't be so hard on yourself. Reward yourself when a task or job in accomplished. Remember that we must have balance in our lives if we are to be human beings instead of human doings.

50) Set Priorities - do first things first!

Procrastination is a common self-defeating behavior. Regular daily tasks are neglected, bills are left unopened, appointments are not kept, and responsibilities forgotten.

Procrastination is like fertilizer for problems. Even little tasks become problems when left unattended and, as time passes, these problems grow quickly like weeds. Soon, little problems become big problems. Problems mount up causing stress until we feel trapped and overwhelmed.

In recovering from self-defeating behaviors, we learn to take responsibility for all our problems and to do whatever footwork is required to solve them as they appear. One simple tool is to make a daily priority list of things that need attention. Unlike like a "Honey Do" list, this list is for your own personal edification and growth.

Make a list each night of the things that need to be taken care of the following day. Be realistic – each item needs to be measurable and attainable (i.e.: instead of "buy a house" try "contact a realtor and make an appointment").

Throughout the day feel free to add to the list. As a matter of fact, if you discover something you take care of that is not on your list, write it on your list and cross it off – this is good practice.

At the end of the day, go through your list and congratulate yourself on your accomplishments. Next, transfer to the top of tomorrow's list the items that didn't get done on today's list.

The more you accomplish, the more motivated to accomplish you become.

51) Perform "Reality Checks" throughout your day. **Chap 19**

Reality Check #1: Awareness/Accountability & Change
(Used to identify and change unwanted feelings.)
A = Awareness/Accountability

"What am I feeling?" I need to identify the feeling I am experiencing. Am I angry, embarrassed, frustrated, afraid, saddened, ashamed, etc.? Once I identify the feeling, I need to identify the motivation behind the feeling –"Why am I feeling this way?" Am I afraid someone will not approve of me, am I upset because I am not getting what I want, etc. Once I identify my motivation, I must accept responsibility for my feeling – I must own it. This is what I feel and this is why.

B = Belief: rational/irrational

Once I've identified my feelings and the motivation which drives each one and have accepted responsibility for each feeling, I must ask myself is it rational for me to feel this way. Is it rational for me to believe I can be happy and serene if I keep this feeling or do I need to change it?

C= Choice: Change/Consequences
                    (pain)   (pain)

Both changing and accepting the consequences involve pain. Change involves short term pain. Consequences involve long-term pain. Change is uncomfortable, but once done, the pain is over with relatively quickly. Accepting the consequences means you keep whatever you have identified until you eventually deal with it.

Reality Check #2: Does It Apply?
(used to check behavior – yours or another's)

When someone gets upset at you or accuses you of something, ask yourself, "Does it apply?" "Has my behavior been such as to warrant such a reaction in this individual." If the answer is, "Yes," then you have the opportunity to set it right – to make apologies or amends. If the answer is, "No," then you are dealing with their issue and it has nothing to do with you. In this instance, their threats and/or accusations are just garbage – and what do you do with garbage? You throw it away.

52) Looking through another's eyes   (see chapter 5)

Success in business is all about relationships, and as mentioned earlier, communication is probably the most important "tool" in any relationship. Without effective communication, even two healthy, loving people will not make it. Remember, you have the right to be heard, to express yourself – your opinions, your feelings, your values. Your wants and needs are important. You deserve respect for who you are. By giving respect to others, you are more deserving of respect for yourself.

The sad fact is, even the most intelligent and talented people have difficulty effectively communicating what they want to convey. One of the purposes of increasing human understanding is to develop constructive and effective ways of sharing and dealing with both positive and negative emotional reactions. Too much of our effort in life is aimed at changing others so we can be happy. We must use that effort to change ourselves from within to be happy.

1) When a person says or does something and it causes me to react in a certain way, I need to understand that just because I reacted in this way doesn't mean the other person intended me to act this way.

2) Rational thinking and logic do not govern feelings. It is important to understand and respect that, no matter what the reason; the feelings another person has are real.

3) We see others the way we "perceive" them, and we perceive others as a direct result of the way we view the world.

4) Until you live their lifetime in their shoes, you cannot know what motivates another person.

5) When we misinterpret another's words or deeds we mistakenly jump to conclusions as to their motives.

6) No one sees reality the way reality really is, we see it the way we are. A person's perception of reality is dictated by their lifetime of experiences, triumphs, failures, challenges, conquests, and their interpretations of these.

EXERCISE: When in disagreement, argument, or confrontation with someone, ask yourself:
  1. Do I really understand this person's point of view? (give feedback and ask for clarification)
  2. Have I made my point of view clear? Does this person fully understand my point of view? (ask for feedback)
  3. How might this person be interpreting this issue?
  4. Why might this person be seeing this issue differently from me?
  5. Does this person have a valid point, depending on the way they see it?
  6. What might be their motivation behind adopting their point of view?
  7. Can I accept that this person has the right to perceive this issue differently from me?
  8. Why do I feel I have to be right or I have to win?
  9. Can I agree to disagree?

---

53) Communication Skills   Chap 11 pg. 120

Communication is the most important tool in any
relationship. Unfortunately, few people know how to
communicate effectively. There are basically five levels of
communication. Few people rarely achieve a level where they are
really sharing anything of themselves. Since I want my
relationships to be healthy, to grow and prosper, it behooves me
to understand these levels and become adept at using them
appropriately.

The Five Levels of Communication

Level One (the lowest level):
Superficial Conversation – Non-communication
At this level there is no real communication of self. I share
nothing of my authenticity as a person. This is the conversation
of casual acquaintances (the club meeting, the neighbor, the
Laundromat). We talk in clichés, such as: "How are you?"
"How is your family?" "Where have you been?" We say things
like, "I like your dress very much." "I hope we can get together
again real soon." "It's really good to see you."

I am careful not to really share anything which is personal
about me. I am content to share pleasantries and so is everyone
else. If I should respond to, "How ya doing?" with a detailed
account of my problems, it would be viewed as a breech of
etiquette. I remain safely in the isolation of my pretense, sham,
and sophistication. It almost seems that everyone in this group
has gathered to be lonely together.

Level Two:
Reporting about others – still nothing about me
At this level I still report nothing about my real self – what
makes me me. I expose nothing about me or what is going on in
my life. I'm still safe from outside scrutiny. I talk about other
people or things, relaying only facts. I give no opinions, no
thoughts, ideas, or feelings – nothing which could be judged.

Level Three:
My Ideas and Opinions

On this level, I am willing to share a little of that which makes me me. I will guardedly offer my ideas and opinions about things. But I will also carefully watch you to discern if you approve or not, and will retreat to safer ground if I detect your disapproval.

Level Four:
How I Feel – My "Gut Level" Emotions

Now, I am willing to risk that which most clearly differentiates and individuates me from others. How I feel about things is what makes me, me. And know this, I am taking a risk – I am exposed to your scrutiny here. I am vulnerable at this point, and if attacked or disapproval is shown, I will retreat and probably never feel safe to return to this level with you.

Level Five: Peak Communication
Complete Openness and Honesty

At this level, I am willing to open my world up to you and let you in. I will be completely open and honest which means I am most vulnerable. This is a precious gift which few people will ever experience. I open my world up to you and I will expect you to open your world up to me. There are five rules of which I need to be aware if a relationship is to maintain this "Peak Level of Communication."

Both parties must:

Rule 1: Must never imply a judgment of the other.
Rule 2: Emotions are not moral; they are neither good nor bad.
Rule 3: Feelings (emotions) must be integrated with the intellect and will.
Rule 4: Emotions must be reported.
Rule 5: Emotions must be reported at the time they are being experienced.

54) Keep an Open Mind

More opportunities have been missed, more lives wasted, and more potential never realized because of unwillingness to consider different opinions, beliefs, or ideas. A closed mind is a lost mind – a dead mind. Just the fact that you've made it this far in this book is an indication you have an open mind. Whether you believe what this book suggests or think it's all just bullshit, at least you've been open enough to consider it.

A wise man or woman will listen and consider before deciding.

55) Put your own welfare first: You're no good for anyone or anything if you're not taking care of yourself.

You're flying along at forty thousand feet. In the seat next to you on your right is your four-year-old son. In the seat to your left is your six-year-old daughter. Suddenly, the plane hits turbulence, the cabin looses pressure, and the oxygen masks drop down. Who do you put the mask on first – your son or your daughter?

The first mask to go on better be your own.

"But that's selfish!"

If you don't put yours on first, you'll be no good for your children. Let's say you put it on your son first. Then you turn to put one on your daughter. As you're putting hers on your head begins to feel light and confused. As you finally get hers fixed, you begin to reach for yours when you notice, just before you pass out, that your son has pulled his off.

56) Orientation Meeting

The "Orientation Meeting" is often a "new hire's" first impression of both me and my department. A good impression will be very helpful in establishing "buy in" and "ownership" in this individual later on.

My four main objectives of the "Orientation Meeting" are:

1) welcome the Individual into the fold,

2) set the stage for Open Heaven,

3) introduce the Individual to the TEAM, and

4) identify early on if an Individual has potential.

Welcoming the individual into the fold is my first opportunity to create a raving fan of this person. I want to alleviate this person's apprehension and offer my trust.

It's critical as manager I understand that all new hires will:

- not be the "orange" they can be,

- feel insecure, intimidated, or even fearful,

- have at least a little bit of Anarchist in them,

- have preconceived ideas about their position which may or may not be true, and

- in most cases, underestimate their abilities.

57) Performance Review Meetings

- New Hire
- Established Staff
  Formal
  Informal
- Setting Fires under Their Feet

This meeting, of course, is used periodically to review the performance of individuals. This may be conducted annually, semi-annually, quarterly, or monthly depending on the industry or necessity. As manager, my job is to make this a positive experience.

Tools for Developing as a Manager

New Hire

I will meet with new hires at least once a month or as necessary. "As necessary" may mean weekly or even semi-weekly. My first few review meetings will not be about performance so much as it will be to see if he or she is settling in all right.

Our first review meeting after the orientation meeting, I want to validate and attempt to alleviate fears and concerns. I tell them that by now they probably feel overwhelmed, stressed, and possibly think, "I can't cut it," (I usually get a body language response affirming this).

I let them know that making mistakes is expected and all right, but hiding mistakes and not learning from mistakes isn't. I impress upon them that mistakes must be reported as soon as they are made.

Established Staff:

A Formal Annual Performance Review Meeting is typically a 1:1 session with just me and the employee sitting down and reviewing where he or she was last year at this time, where they wanted to go this last year, if they got there – then "why" they got there, and if they didn't get there – then "why" they didn't.

Together, we evaluate the employee's growth in a number of areas:

1) Performance

2) Buy-In

3) Ownership of Their Position

4) Career Mindedness

5) Identifying and Serving Their Customer

6) Effectivity

7) Maintaining Standards

8) Setting and Monitoring Goals

9) CORE Competencies

Together, we rate the employee on a scale of 1 – 5 with 1 being "Needs a Lot of Help," 3 being "Thoroughly and Satisfactorily Meeting Requirements of the position," and 5 being "Far Exceeds Requirements."

An Informal Performance Review Meeting is typically a 1:1, or individual, session in which we need to explore a problem or potential problem that has become apparent.

By reading body language, I should be able to tell where an individual is at when they enter my office. I need to "cut the crap" immediately because neither one of us have time to waste. Once again, my objective is to assist them in reaching their objectives, or goals, and I need to remind this individual that we need to get real and get down to the business of helping one another.

NOTE: I always email each individual, summarizing the objective and outcome of the meeting and thanking them for their participation. I then put a copy of the email in their personnel file for documentation and later reference.

---

58) "Setting Fires Under Their Feet" Meeting

This is a meeting in which performance has slumped and a "reality check" is in order. This meeting is facilitated as a group session, which can even include an entire department.

The purpose of this type of meeting is to:

1) Recognize that an "obvious problem" exists,

2) Identify what the "core problem" is,

3) Identify consequences if problem is not resolved,

4) Uncover solution options, and

5) Initiate action.

One way to facilitate this meeting is to float a "doom balloon," read body language, and then "peal the onion". This method is most effective when members of staff are already aware of their delinquent behavior (see example, chapter 16).

But there are times when everyone has no idea anything is wrong and believe they are doing well. This is when I want to guide them through a process which will inspire them to participate in the solution.

Before I begin, I need to inspect what I expect. Is what I expect realistic? If I inspect it and still believe it is, then I proceed.

> **Note:** Seldom is an "obvious problem" the "core problem." In effect, I sometimes need to peal a problem like I peal an onion if I am to discover the core (real) problem. Sometimes, there are many steps between the obvious problem and the core problem.

> **NOTE:** I always email each individual, summarizing the objective and outcome of the meeting and thanking them for their participation. I then put a copy of the email in their personnel file for documentation and later reference.

59) Superstar Review Meetings

Superstars are often the "Lost Children" of business. Because they shine, everything appears to be going great. A major mistake many managers make is not nurturing their superstars.

One problem with superstars is because they do well, more is expected of them. This, in itself, is stress producing and will often deter a superstar from seeking needed help. They come to believe they're not allowed to make mistakes. They push themselves hard and they beat themselves hard when they don't live up to expectations. Without attention and guidance, superstars will inevitably suffer from either mediocrity, or even worse, burnout.

When a Superstar is doing well

When a superstar is doing well, I, of course, only want to nurture and assist. I am there mainly just to listen. I'm not going to tell them what to do, if they are already doing exceptionally well. Many managers feel they must introduce new ideas and procedures to coach the individual on to even greater heights. Or, they feel it's their duty as management to find some area to criticize.

All this does is "piss off" the superstar because this is a person who already knows what to do. After all, they're doing it!

My job is to get out of their way and let them do what they were hired to do. I do want to:

1) validate their success,

2) look for signs of mediocrity or burnout,

3) reaffirm that I am here to provide assistance whenever they may require it, and

4) inspect what they're doing so I may learn and pass the information on to others.

When a Superstar is in a slump

Superstars fall into ruts at times and become tired, bored, antsy, and just want a change. But superstars are often overly hard on themselves. It's important to identify the "core problem" in a situation like this early on.

My basic job is to support and encourage, but I also want to walk my superstar through a reality check (see "List of Tools" in Index) to identify where the real problem lies.

NOTE: I always email each individual, summarizing the objective and outcome of the meeting and thanking them for their participation. I then put a copy of the email in their personnel file for documentation and later reference.

---

60) Clear the Air Meeting

In monitoring the pulse of staff (chapter 16), there may be times when I notice a "rain cloud" developing in Open Heaven. It's important I identify the cause and dissipate this "rain cloud" before it matures into a thunderhead. Most rain clouds are precipitated by personalities and politics.

Some examples of rain clouds include:

- **Unexpressed Grievances**

- **Emotional Involvement** (fraternization)

- **Rumors**

- **Misinformation**

- **Misperceptions of Open Heaven**

Pre – 1:1 temperature taking. This is a pre-meeting in which I meet privately 1:1 with a few key personnel to gather different perceptions of what is going on.

A "Clear the Air" Meeting is a "reality check" / "get back on track," group meeting in which everyone who possibly could be affected is included.

At this meeting, I am going to facilitate while the group does the work. The idea is to guide them through a process in which they police themselves. I only allow one person to speak at a time.

There are 3 main objectives in "clearing the air;"

1) **give information,**

2) **stop speculation, and**

3) **get back on track.**

61) Red Flag Meeting

Typically, a red flag meting is a 1:1 session, expressing concern for an individual. Whenever I notice red flags in a person such as;

> Self-defeating Behaviors,
>
> Cognitive Distortions,
>
> Attitudes that lead to Mediocrity,
>
> Complacency, or
>
> Signs of Burnout,

it's necessary I meet with that person, make them aware of what I am seeing, express my concern, get clarification and feedback, and offer support. Since I will notice red flags in an individual long before he or she does (can't see the forest for the trees), it's important I bring it to their attention early so we can identify the problem and get back on track.

First, I want to validate the person as a valued person and employee.

Second, I lay out the problem as I see it.

Third, I want to identify the core problem by offering the employee an opportunity to get anything they may need to off their chest.

Fourth, I wait for a response.

I want the employee to:

1. recognize and admit his behavior

2. open him up if something is bothering him

3. work with me in coming up with some "solution options."

NOTE: I always email each individual, summarizing the objective and outcome of the meeting and thanking them for their participation. I then put a copy of the email in their personnel file for documentation and later reference.

---

62) Conflict Mediation and Resolution

This is a situation in which two or more members of staff are angry and/or confrontational toward one another.

This process involves the following steps:

1. **Setting the stage**

2. **Explaining my position as facilitator**

3. **Setting the ground rules for this meeting**

   - The parties are not allowed to speak to one another only to me and only when I ask them to. (Later, they may be able to speak to one another, but only if I allow them.)

   - No interrupting. (Each person will have an opportunity to speak as much as they like, but only when I have given them permission.)

   - No name calling.

   - No verbal abuse.

   - No physical violence.

   - If I feel a person's behavior is "out-of-hand" or abusive, I will stop the discussion and warn the individual. If the behavior continues, that person will be asked to leave and we remaining parties will continue without them.

   - No one is allowed to repeat anything said at this meeting outside of this meeting.

   - Both parties will agree to remain in this meeting until the issue is resolved.

4. **Peeling the onion to discover the issue**

5. **Getting each person to see the other's perspective**

6. **Getting out of the problem and into the solution**

7. **Obtaining a commitment**

63) Come to Jesus meeting

A "Come to Jesus" meeting is used for gross or flagrant violations of standards or CORE Competencies. This type of meeting is used after an individual, or group of individuals, have already been informed or warned of a behavior or attitude which needs correction, but the individual continues to commit the same offense.

This meeting has usually already been preceded by a "Red Flag," "Performance," or "Setting Fires Under Their Feet" meeting. In essence, this is a "second chance" for the individual to get on track. I want to "check" my emotion at the door and I want to "cut through the fluff."

At this meeting, I will take the lead – I control the meeting.

I want to:

- Inform the individual of the problem.

- Remind them that this problem has been previously addressed.

- Inform them that there is no possible excuse for this behavior continuing.

- Ask them why this problem has not been corrected. (It's important I keep them on track and not allow them to avoid taking responsibility by blaming or rationalizing.)

- Let them know the consequence if this problem is not resolved immediately.

- Give them the choice to comply or leave and then ask what their decision is.

NOTE: Once again, I email the individual, summarizing the objective and outcome of the meeting and thanking them for their participation. I then put a copy of the email in their personnel file for documentation and later reference.

---

64) Termination meeting

Depending on the circumstances, an individual may be terminated for many reasons. For our purposes, we'll look at two basic instances: immediate termination for committing a serious infraction and termination for inability to perform.

Immediate termination for committing a serious infraction

Any individual committing a serious infraction which jeopardizes the health or well-being of himself or others must be dealt with quickly and definitively. Such infractions include, but are not limited to: theft of company or coworkers' property, the use and/or distribution of pornographic material, bringing a weapon to work, and threatening or committing violence – in short, basically any illegal activity. One of the most serious infractions concerns discovering an anarchist in my department (see "Anarchists," chapter 19). Anarchists must be weeded out immediately.

When terminating an employee in this situation:

- Contact all necessary management.
- Assess whether the individual is a threat to himself/herself or others, and if he/she is, contact police, internal security personnel, and get coworkers to safety.
- Notify police of any illegal act.
- Have individual accompanied by internal security personnel (if available) or by at least two members of management (as witnesses) until he leaves the building.
- Remain calm – respond, do not react.
- Inform individual his employment is terminated and explain the nature of the infraction.
- Allow the individual to ask questions, but maintain control of the situation. Do not allow the individual to misdirect or manipulate.

- Accompany individual as he packs his personal items from his work station.

- Collect all company property from the individual.

- Escort the individual from the premises and inform him that he is not allowed back on the premises, and should he appear, the police will be called.

- Inform individual that any further contact will be with upper management, the legal department, or attorneys, and he should direct all calls to them.

- Give the individual the appropriate contact numbers.

It is extremely important to make the individual's exit as quickly and quietly as possible so as not to disrupt the work environment. This is particularly important when terminating an anarchist. The best way to do this is during a meeting where everyone, or most everyone, is required to attend. By the time the meeting is over, the individual should be gone.

Termination for inability to perform

As the term implies, this is a meeting in which I am going to terminate an individual because they are just not able to "cut it" or they couldn't care less about the job they're doing. Either way, this individual is costing the business time and energy, affecting the work environment, and consuming company resources. This doesn't mean they've done anything wrong, but this person needs to go.

It's important, as manager, that I:

1. Make termination a positive experience.
2. Set up proper documentation to support the termination.
3. Refrain from using the terms, "fire, fired, or firing."
4. Treat the individual with respect and dignity.

Tools for Developing as a Manager

How to terminate an individual for inability to perform

Schedule the meeting early in the week (to allow the individual to start a job search immediately). I also recommend the meeting be scheduled early in the day.

Include the individual's supervisor and a Human Resources representative (always have a witness).

All present should sit on the same level with no one between the employee and the door.

Keep your emotions in check – respond don't react.

Be open, honest, direct, and compassionate.

- Inform the individual they are terminated. Let them know that you and the company regret this decision, but that it is for the good of the individual as well as the company.

- Explain the reason(s) for this decision. This is usually not a surprise for the individual. If proper reviews, Red Flag, and Come to Jesus meetings have been conducted the employee should already know they are not meeting standards.

- Validate the individual's strengths, abilities, and talents. Assure them that they are much better suited for another position or field where their abilities would be better utilized. Let them know that remaining at a job where they constantly struggle just to get by, and where their real talents are not being developed only traps them in a life of stress and mediocrity.

- Allow the individual to ask questions. It is all right to engage in conversation for clarification, but be aware that the individual may begin to make excuses, try to manipulate for another chance, and even get angry.

- Remember, the decision to terminate has already been made. This is not a negotiation meeting.

Note: Once they have been informed of termination, the individual must never be left alone. Even the most accepting employee can suddenly turn resentful or even hostile.

- Offer (don't force) discussion on what field or job where their talents may best be used and in which they would have a higher opportunity for success. Offer discussion on resources for job or career searching, possible schooling, and degrees or certification.

- Ask the individual to return all company property.

- Ask the individual for computer and email passwords and any codes for cell phones or any other piece of equipment to which another employee will need access.

- Allow the individual to choose who at the meeting they would like to accompany them to Human Resources or Personnel to complete necessary arrangements for payroll (unused vacation time, accrued sick time, advanced payments, unpaid commissions, expense account reimbursement, etc.), benefits (health, life, retirement, etc.), and COBRA (Consolidated Omnibus Budget Reconciliation Act of 1980) information. The individual should also give written permission for you to provide reference information should you be contacted by potential employers.

Note: Contact HR or Personnel beforehand and have them ready to receive the individual. I don't want a person sitting around stewing, becoming frustrated, irritable, and possibly causing a scene. The objective is to get the individual out smoothly and quickly. Once a person is told he is terminated, show them respect and dignity, but do not allow them to loiter. The longer they remain, the more sympathy and support they will get from well-meaning rescuers.

- Allow the individual to choose whether they would like to collect their personal belongings now or after hours. If they choose now, have someone accompany them.

I want a terminated employee to have an opportunity to say good-bye to peers and colleagues if the individual is positive and appreciative of their experience of Open Heaven (and most are), but once again, my primary duty is to protect my staff.

65) Interview Questions (in Starting Up a Department)

A "Manager from the Heart" hires to the position, while keeping the "bigger picture" in mind. I look for someone who will be compatible to working in an "Open Heaven" environment. I want someone who is teachable. I can do almost anything with someone who is teachable.

First of all, I am the one who interviews the individual, not someone from personnel. It's important I chose my staff and not someone who will never see them again and has no idea what I want in my staff.

The interview process itself is an invaluable opportunity for me to:

1) get an understanding of who this individual is and where they want to go,

2) evaluate if this person will be able to function in an "Open Heaven" environment,

3) discern if this individual is "teachable,"

4) and most importantly, bond with the individual if I deem them appropriate for my staff.

If I believe this individual will be a good fit for my department, the interview process enables me to begin the "bonding process." I will learn about the individual and they will learn about me. I will begin a "preliminary initiation" to the concept of "Open Heaven" and what my role as manager will be.

But how can I tell if an individual has what I'm looking for? I will ask open-ended questions, float balloons, watch for red flags, read body language, and peal the onion. I will first want to invite the person in (preferably into my office) and make him feel comfortable and important (see page 180).

The following are only suggestions for questions you may find helpful in determining whether an individual is someone you will want to invest in.

1. What brings you to <u>the name of your organization</u> ?
(example: What brings you to <u>HeartStandards?</u>) Of course, this person is looking for a job, but this is a way to get a feel of what he knows about your company. This question is also a "lead in" to the next question.

2. What is your understanding of what we do at HeartStandards?
This is a straight on follow-up question to the first question. This allows the interviewee to give and in-depth account of what he knows and also allows me to see how well this individual has done his homework.

3. Why do you want to work for us?
This allows me to check for motivation. By reading body language, I'm able to discern if this is practiced or genuine.

4. If you were hired, how do you see yourself benefitting <u>HeartStandards?</u>
This question gives the individual an opportunity to explain his attributes and skills, and again, his understanding of what you are looking for in this position. Is this person looking at the bigger picture? Has this person done their homework?

5. What exactly makes you think you would do well at this particular position?
This question is "position specific." Will the individual just repeat what he answered in the previous question or will he get

specific? Usually, the individual will expound on his experiences at this point.

6. Tell me about your experience in this field.

This is a "fish or cut bait" question. This allows me to discern the individual's honesty. By reading body language, I'm able to decipher if his reply is rehearsed or genuine.

7. If you were hired, do you see yourself staying in this position indefinitely?

This indicates the individual's motivation.

8. Tell me about yourself:

Of course, this is the most often asked question in any interview, and yet, few interviewers really know why they ask it. What exactly are you looking for when asking this question? Personally, I look for: a) does this individual have a sense of themselves (purpose), b) are they full of themselves, c) do they have a sense of direction (where they want to go), d) can they perceive a "bigger picture," and e) are they "teachable."

9. Do you consider yourself successful in your personal life?

This is a "lead in" question. Of course, this person will answer, "yes," at which you counter with "how?" This question gives me a good sense of what this person values and whether they are just telling me what they think I want to hear.

10. What have you done in this past year to nurture success in your personal life?

This gives me an idea of the individual's ability to have vision and the willingness to work toward it.

11. Do you consider yourself successful in your professional life?

Of course, this person will answer, "yes," at which you counter with "how do you feel you are successful?"

12. What have you done in this past year to nurture success in your professional life?

Again, this gives me an idea of the individual's ability to have vision and the willingness to work toward it.

13. What would you say your greatest strength is?

This allows the person to express their personal "selling points."

14. What would previous employers say your greatest strengths are?

This question gives the individual an opportunity to get honest and let's me compare this answer with the answer to #13.

15. What would your coworkers say are your greatest strengths?

This will give me insight to how this person thinks others see him.

16. What motivates you to be your best?

This is indicative of where this person's priorities lay.

17. Do you think you might be overqualified for this position?

If so, then why does this person want it? This is a warning sign for me. This person will probably only be around long enough to get a better job.

18. Would your particular skills or talents be better suited for another position? If so, what?

This gives me an idea of what position this person is really interested in.

19. What would previous employers say are your weaknesses?

This gives me an idea how honest and forthcoming this person is.

20. What would your coworkers say your weaknesses are?
This gives me an idea how "in tuned" with others he is.

21. What do you think your weaknesses are?
This tells me how "in tune" with himself he is.

22. What have you done to resolve your weaknesses?
This tells me how aware and proactive this person is in their personal growth?

23. Why did you leave your last place of employment?
From this question, I should be able to detect levels honesty, culpability, openness, resentment, and/or responsibility. This can be a "Red Flag" if, by reading body language, I feel this person is being dishonest.

24. Have you ever been fired or asked to resign from a position? And if so, why?
Again, I should be able to detect levels honesty, culpability, openness, resentment, and/or responsibility.

25. How would you describe your work ethic?
This tells me how this person sees himself.

26. What's most important to you, the work or the money?
I am looking for someone who is honest and teachable.

27. Do you feel you get along well with others? And if so, how?
I expect everyone to say yes, but I find they have to give some thought to "how?" This question clues me in to what they think of their coworkers.

28. Do you consider yourself a team player? And if so, why?
Again I expect yes, but "why" should give me insight to what role they usually assume.

29. When working on a team project, what position on the team are you most comfortable with? Why are you comfortable?

This should give me some insight as to whether they are a leader or a follower and how much of a role (and responsibility) they are willing to assume.

30. What frustrates you about working on "team projects?"

This will give them an opportunity to complain about previous projects they've worked on. This should give insight to how much of a team player they really are and how much responsibility they're willing to accept.

31. What frustrates you about coworkers?

You can tell a lot about a person by what they dislike in others.

32. What problems have you experienced with coworkers?

This can tell me if they have a tendency to blame others, own up to their part in a problem, and whether they accept (or shirk) responsibility.

33. What have you learned from these experiences?

This tells me the level of honesty and insight of this individual. By reading body language, I can gage truthfulness.

34. How would you apply that knowledge to this position?

This will tell me how much this person really knows about the position they are interviewing for. It is also a good indicator how adept this individual is at applying what they have learned.

35. What type of individual would you not be able to work with?

Again this is a good indication of what this individual is really like. Most people do not like to be around people who exhibit qualities they dislike in themselves.

36. What frustrates you about supervisors or managers?

This can be a good indicator of the individual's willingness to follow direction, comply with standards, and interact with others.

37. What problems have you experienced with supervisors or managers?

Again, I'm looking for honesty and willingness to accept direction. This also indicates the individual's ability to resolve differences.

38. What have you learned from these experiences?

Can this individual learn from their mistakes or do they play the victim role.

39. How might you apply this knowledge to this new position?

Is this person able to change behaviors when they are unhealthy?

40. What has disappointed you about your jobs in the past?

I'm looking for what this person expects in a job. Are they willing to work or just show up. Are they Career-Minded or Job-Minded?

41. What have you learned from these disappointments?

Again, are they able to apply what they have learned?

42. What would be the ideal job for you?

Again, are they Career-Minded or Job-Minded?

43. What would you consider your ideal workplace environment to be?

I want to know if this individual lives is reality. Are they willing to contribute or just take?

44. What exactly would you be looking for in this position?

This ties the previous eighteen questions in to pinpoint what this person expects working for me. I'm looking to see if they will "fit," not only in this position, but in an "Open Heaven" environment.

45. How long would you expect to work for us if you were hired?

It this just temporary for this individual? I'm looking for a long-term "fit." If I'm going through the time and expense of training and mentoring this individual, I want it to be worthwhile. Someone who is planning to go off to college at the end of the summer or get married to somebody with two kids and be a stay-at-home parent won't cut it.

46. What salary are you looking for?

This will give me an idea whether or not they are living in reality, undervalue (or overvalue) their self, have done their homework, and are motivated.

47. Would you be willing to work evenings or weekends? What about overtime?

This clues me in to their motivation (their willingness) to do whatever it takes. If they're not willing and the position doesn't require it, I could hire them anyway. But this question still gives me awareness of their limitations.

48. Would you be willing to relocate if necessary?

Again, this question testifies to this person's level of commitment.

49. If necessary, are you willing to put the welfare of the company ahead of your interests?

I'm looking for honesty and willingness to be a team player. By reading body language, it's easy to discern when this person is full of bull.

50. Is the work or money more important to you?
If the money is more important, then they're looking for a job. If the job is more important, they're either lying or they're looking for a career. I'm looking for someone who sees them both important.

51. What are the qualities you would like to see in your boss?
This can tell me a lot about a person's insight, work ethic, and previous relationships with bosses.

52. Tell me about a time when you made a suggestion that changed your workplace?
This can show whether they've ever had "ownership" of a position or "buy in" to a workplace environment.

53. What are some examples of your ability to work under pressure?
This is an opportunity for them to show off by recanting some of their attributes. It also gives me a good idea what they consider "stress."

54. What do you find is your biggest problem when working under pressure?
After they've "shown off," it's time to get real. If they claim to not have any problems under pressure then they're either lying or living in denial. If they claim to thrive under pressure, I wonder if they also create pressure just so they can thrive.

For interviewing managers:

55. Describe your management style.
Many managers aren't aware they have a style – they just do what they do. Depending on how involved the answer is tells me how aware this individual is about what they do. Every good manager has given this some thought, has tested different styles, and has worked on improving his or her style. A good manager is constantly "honing" his or her craft.

56. Under what circumstances would you be willing to change your management style?

I'm looking for someone who is willing to try new things in an effort to improve themselves. I am not looking for someone who is entrenched and fears change.

57. What is your greatest satisfaction as a manager?

Is this individual bottom-line oriented or people oriented? Of course the "bottom-line" is important, but it's your greatest asset (your people) that makes your bottom-line what it is.

I'm looking for someone whose focus is on his or her people.

58. What is your greatest frustration as a manager?

If this person's greatest satisfaction as manager is his or her people, then I will expect this will also be their greatest frustration as well.

If this person is bottom-line oriented, then depending how much frustration they display toward their people will tell you how "people oriented" they are. A manager who can only complain about staff has no people skills, and thus, no ability to manage people.

59. How do you typically resolve disputes between others?

Again, does this individual have people skills? Do they actually resolve disputes or do they just order those involved to stop? Ordering to stop only makes the problem worse by sending it underground where it will fester and eventually affect others.

60. How many employees have you fired?

I prefer someone who has experienced the firing process. If an individual has been a manager for a while and has not fired anyone – I want to know why. Does this individual fear confrontation?

On the other hand, if an individual has fired an inordinate amount of people, I also want to know why. Either this person is poor at hiring qualified individuals or they are poor at guiding, mentoring, and managing.

61. How does firing someone make you feel?

I want someone who doesn't enjoy firing someone, can empathize with the individual, but also realizes it's the best thing for him, the business, and the person being fired.

62. How many other jobs are you applying for?

This tells me how serious this individual is, who and what they think they are suited for, and their level of confidence. If they are applying for other positions, I will be concerned with why they think they will be satisfied with this particular position with us.

63. If you were hiring a person for this position, what's the main question you would ask?

This gives me an idea how this individual thinks of their feet, how they view this position, and their style of managing.

64. What has frustrated you about upper management?

This tells me what problems this person has had with upper management. I can also get an idea if this person is an innovative thinker who has been stifled or if they are just defiant.

65. Do you know anyone employed by us?

Some companies have a policy against family members being employed at the same facility. Besides this, I can tell something about the individual by who he or she associates with.

66. What do you need to work on professionally?

Now is an opportunity for this individual to get real and impress me. If they are honest, they will come up with at least a few things. If they say, "nothing," or are superficial, they damage their credibility with me.

If they are real, speak openly, and have some good points, they greatly enhance their credibility with me. I can't work with someone who is perfect, but I will often be willing to go the distance with someone who is authentic.

67. What makes you the best person for this job?

Again, this question gives this individual the opportunity to get real. Plus, I am sometimes surprised with insight, which I hadn't thought of before.

EXERCISE:

a) Break up into groups of three and take turns: one person play the interviewer, one the interviewee, and one the observer.

b) Choose 20 questions and be prepared to share with the entire group why you pick them.

Tools for Developing Staff

66) Floating Balloons   (chap 16)   pg. 207

　　　Floating balloons is an effective tool when "reading the pulse" of either an individual or my department. Floating balloons is a technique used to produce an emotional response in an individual or group of individuals. This technique is simple.

　　　First I make an unexpected, out-of-the-ordinary statement, catching people off guard, and then I simply wait for a response. By observing the body language of my employee(s) when floating a particular balloon, I get an idea of how certain ideas, concepts, attitudes, behaviors, or issues will be received or should be addressed. Since body language is a natural, unconscious physical response to an emotion, it is often a more reliable indicator of people's true feelings than their words.

Floating balloons is effective when:

- I want feedback to a new idea or concept,
- I need to "test the atmosphere" of the department,
- I believe an individual is not being honest with me, or
- an individual has a flat affect (see Body Language).

Basically, there are three types of balloons:

- **Weather Balloons,**
- **Carrot Balloons, and**
- **Doom Balloons**

Weather Balloons: A weather balloon tells me which way the wind is blowing concerning a certain subject. This is when I announce a new concept or process, let an individual or individuals think about it, and then wait for feedback. In other words, this balloon allows me to test the atmosphere of an individual or my department.

Carrot Balloons: A carrot balloon is an incentive balloon. This is when I validate the work an individual or group of individuals are doing and then offer an incentive (dangle a carrot) for continued performance. A carrot balloon tells me who's "on board" with a particular idea or process and alerts me to problems and potential problems in culture and individuals.

Doom Balloons: A doom balloon is where I drop a bomb, letting an individual, or group of individuals, know that standards or performance is not on track with goals and redirection of process needs to take place.

I do not expect to resolve an issue when I drop a bomb. I want them to feel the fallout and reflect on their behavior.

EXERCISE:

#1. Sales are up. Billing is behind. You assess the "primary problem" to be your sales reps are not completing their required paperwork in a timely manner. Give an example of a balloon you would float. What will you look for when floating this balloon?

#2. The manager of another department is advocating some of his staff's duties be reassigned to your department. Give an example of balloon you would float. What will you look for when floating this balloon?

#3. You hear a member of your staff is disgruntled over the promotion of a peer. Give an example of balloon you would float. What will you look for when floating this balloon?

#4. Support staff are dragging their feet in servicing the sales reps. Your sales reps are resentful and complaining. Your support staff complains the sales reps are demanding and unappreciative. Give an example of a balloon you would float. What will you look for when floating this balloon?

---

67) Who is my Customer?   (chapter #2)

In servicing a customer, there will be times when you feel like "this ain't my job."   In times like these, ask yourself the following questions:

1) Can this person benefit from my services?

2) Does this person require my services?

3) Can I service this person effectively?

4) Is it my responsibility to service this person?

5) How best can I service this person?

If you answer "Yes" to any one of these questions, then this individual is your customer. Even if you answer "No" to number 4, your job then is to service this person by handing him or her over to the appropriate staff.

68) Are they a Raving Fan?   (chapter # 8)
If not – then why not?
What haven't I done?

Raving fans result from a person living the principles and concepts described in this book. It is essential I educate each of my employees on what raving fans are, the benefits of having raving fans, and how to create raving fans. Once an individual understands the significance of raving fans, he or she may need help in creating them.

My first step is educating my employee on the process described in chapter 8:

- Set the example. Be honest and open in all your dealings.
- Stop and give them attention
- Let them know they are important
- Listen!

- Ask for and give feedback.

- Share the praise.

- Be the Orange – Exhibit the CORE Competencies

Once the individual understands the process, my next step is to involve them in role-playing. Role-playing is a powerful tool to get someone out of their comfort zone while in a safe setting. This allows them to make mistakes, receive guidance, and most of all, practice.

Learning to change old behavior takes repetition, and it is better to perform repetition in role-playing than on the customer. At first the employee is usually hesitant and falters, but with practice, their comfort level will increase and they learn to be themselves.

Being myself is the key to creating raving fans. At first, I may feel uncomfortable and like I am trying to manipulate someone. But as I practice the process, it becomes second nature to me and I begin to realize there is really nothing manipulative about the process at all. In fact, what I am really doing is discarding old manipulative behaviors and replacing them with a more genuine me.

People aren't stupid; they sense manipulation and that's why when they meet someone who is genuine they are attracted to that person.

EXERCISE: Remember them!

If your staff are important then don't forget them. Little things which mean something to them should mean something to you (birthdays, anniversaries, son's graduation, etc.). Set your email calendar to send you an email warning a few days before an event and give a personalized card (no secretary signing) with a $5 Gift Card to Starbucks or whatever they're interested in (in other words, Know Your Customer).

Stop at a stationary store and pick up twenty assorted blank cards. Periodically, fill out the card saying how much you

---

appreciate a person's work and them as an individual. Then sign it, "A Friend." No name. Address it to them and casually leave it on their desk when no one is watching.

69) Setting the Foundation (Ground Rules)

- What's expected of a person as an individual.
- What's expected of a person as a "member of the family."
- My function as manager.

It is important for an employee to understand that this work environment is going to be unlike any other work environment they have experienced. And because this environment will be different, they will need assistance in understanding what is expected of them as an individual, what is expected of them as a "member of the family," and what my function is as manager.

What's expected as an individual
It's my job to let them know that what is expected of them as an individual is to be open and honest in all their dealings, to ask for help, to be willing to learn, to grow, to change, and to learn responsibility for themselves as a human being. They must be willing to "wrap their brain" around new and unusual concepts. They must be willing to believe in themselves.

What's expected as a "member of the family"
What is expected of them as a "member of the family" is to respect the inner dignity of each and every other family member, to accept that they are not alone, and understand that what affects one effects all. They are expected to honor themselves by, first and foremost, honoring others.
- No disrespecting
- No backbiting
- No gossiping
- No alliances
- No sabotaging

My function as manager.
I tell them that my function as manager is to "serve" them. I will not judge; I will not manipulate; and I will not coerce. My main objective is to provide them with everything within my power to allow them to grow to their full potential. And once they reach their potential, my function then is to guide them in discovering a new and even higher potential.

It is important that the individual hear me say these words, but it is imperative that I believe these words. If I don't believe these words, then I shouldn't say them. The individual must hear these words come out of my mouth. These words will sound "corny" to them, and at first, to me too. But that's OK.

70) 24 Hour "I'm Sorry" Reprieve.

Set a period of 24 hours in which you are not allowed to say, "I'm sorry." Ask your friends or coworkers to assist you in reminding you if you slip. It's interesting to discover how many times throughout a day we say, "I'm sorry." Are we really sorry? If not, then why say it?

For someone who finds themselves continually saying they're sorry it's important to realize that, "I'm sorry," loses all meaning. Instead of a sign of consideration it actually turns into self-deprecating self-talk which will keep shame spirals in motion.

71) Inspect what You Expect

Accept rather than Expect. Expectations are resentments waiting to happen. By expecting certain things, I will often set myself up for disappointment. (Explained in chapters 17 & 18)

72) Body Language   (see chapter 15)

The ability to read and interpret body language is a powerful tool for any manager. Between 60-80% of the message we send is communicated through body language. If I can become proficient at reading body language I am much more capable to correctly interrupt what an individual is saying and thus confirm validity of information and discern problems.

Reading body language is an art in itself. For an in-depth study of reading body language, see chapter 15, pages 183 – 193 in the text. For our purposes here, we will look at two problem areas.

Control Freaks

Some people have an inner "need" to feel in control. This "need" is usually motivated by insecurity and fear. Oddly enough, many control freaks do not realize they are controlling. Most believe they are helping.

Even with good intentions, and most do have good intentions, controllers will dominate, not only others, projects, and meetings, but all areas of the department. The old adage, "Give him an inch and he'll take a mile" is true for controllers. This stifles creativity, causing dissension and alliances among staff.

A couple of cues to recognize controllers are:

- A tendency to interrupt before another is finished.

- A tendency to over-talk another.

- Having a particular seat where they always sit at meetings and a tendency to protect their "usual place."

- Will spread binders, notebooks, papers, folders, etc., out in front of themselves at a meeting to "mark-off" their territory.

- Always having a "better" idea, which often plays off another person's idea.

- Always having to have the last word.

- They hate being interrupted, but interrupt others because their idea is better.

- Always offering suggestions or advice on how others should think or behave or do their work.

- Have a tendency to subtly, and almost covertly, take over the running of a meeting.

- Always has "constructive" criticism about everything and everyone.

- Has a tendency to invade personal space to make another person feel uncomfortable and defensive.

EXERCISE:

1. once everyone is seated at a meeting, ask a suspected controller to change seats

2. ask the individual who they think has the best idea

3. ask the individual to just listen during this meeting without saying anything

---

Lying

Lying is stressful for the liar due to the individual's need to monitor 1) their story, 2) eye contact, 3) facial expression, 4) tone of voice, 5) body position and movements, and 6) general attitude all at the same time. This multitasking makes it extremely difficult for anyone to keep track of everything at once and still listen effectively to another person.

Sometimes it is difficult to know when or if an individual is lying. When accused, an innocent person will become offensive while a guilty person will become defensive. By being aware of some of the following points, I have better insight whether to investigate a person's story further.

1) Their Story. A liar's story is designed to convince me of "their" version of the truth. It will often be elaborate, halting, and sprinkled with some truths to illustrate authenticity. When interrupted, most liars will usually start over as if repeating a rehearsed script.

2) Eye contact. Liars avoid or force eye contact as though I will see the truth in their eyes. If eye contact is forced, a person will not be able to maintain it for long and will break it off. An individual may have a tendency to blink at a faster pace than normal and their pupils will tend to be more dilated.

3) Facial expression will become stiff and forced, as the individual attempts to "create" a convincing, emotional expression, which is opposite what they are really feeling. When lying, I have to hide deceit, fear, guilt, and shame by forcing a sincere "happy" face. Often, it is much easier to just maintain a "Flat Affect" or deadpan, poker-faced expression.

My expression will be limited to mouth movement only. Because my smile is fake, it will not look natural. Only the muscles around the mouth are involved.

4) Tone of voice will often not match verbal statements. A liar may clear their throat a number of times in preparation for finding the right tone.

5) Body position and gestures will also be stiff and limited. Liars tend to touch their face and neck more than usual. They are also inclined to scratch neck, nose, and ears.

6) General attitude of liars is one of defensiveness, insecurity, and impatience. They do not like to face questioners and will often turn their face or body away. They may use sarcasm or humor to deflect a subject. A liar will often repeat my words to answer my question and is more apt to use formal English.

The importance of knowing when someone is lying is that it alerts me that there is something significantly wrong in Open Heaven. I need to address this behavior with the individual in private to get a clear understanding of this person's motivation behind the lie. Then we need to either do some serious work or I need to let this individual go.

EXERCISE: When suspecting that someone is lying:

1. ask them to look you in the eyes

2. change the subject and see if they follow or want to change it back

3. ask them to repeat part of their story they shared in the beginning

4. when detecting a discrepancy in their story, ask them to explain

5. ask them if they are being truthful

73) "Listen" to people   (see chapter 8)

Nothing shows validation and respect more than listening. Unfortunately, most of us are too busy planning what we want to say next to listen effectively and we lose much of the meaning others are trying to convey. When I really listen to what you have to say I am validating that you are important – your opinions, thoughts, and ideas.

Hearing and listening are two separate things. When I hear something – I am a spectator. When I listen – I participate. Listening is an art which must be cultivated if it is to be effective.

Effective Listening Entails

Full eye contact: when two people are looking at one another, each knows the other is paying attention. Sometimes, more is told by the eyes than by the words.

Appropriate time and place: it's difficult to really listen to someone when you are in a busy, crowded room. If you want to listen to what someone has to say, ask them to step outside or invite them into your office. This demonstrates a willingness to hear and respect for the other person.

If a person IS important then don't treat them like they're not – don't take them for granted.

Tools for Developing Staff

Free from outside distractions: take them to your office and put the "Do Not Disturb" sign on your door or ask your secretary to "hold" all calls. Ask them to sit appropriately close and facing you. Pardon yourself for a second while you put your desk phone on mute and turn off your cell phone. Close and set aside any files or work on your desk or both of you sit away from your desk and face one another. (Make sure this person sees you making these preparations. This behavior demonstrates that you are serious about giving him your full attention.)

Avoid "Why?" questions; use "Where?" "What?" "When?" "How?" questions: try to avoid "why questions" as much as possible. "Why questions" usually question validity and prompt defensiveness. "Where, what, when, and how questions," on the other hand usually help get to the "meat" of what the other person is trying to convey and connotes an attempt to understand.

Ask For and Give Feedback: Ask questions: Ask for clarification: Reflect what you heard him/her say. Let them know you heard them and that you want to understand.

Good Feedback Is:

Descriptive, not evaluative or judgmental; specific, not general.

Sensitive to both receiver and giver.

To check for understanding.

To check out assumptions

To share observations

To share how I am affected by you and/or your behavior.

Blocks to Listening

Making assumptions that you know what the other person is meaning.

Hidden agendas detract you from hearing what the other person is saying and keeps you focused only on your agenda. This shows disrespect for the other person.

Preparing your own reply while the other person is speaking prevents you from absorbing their meaning. It also makes you look like an idiot when your reply has nothing to do with what they're saying.

> **EXERCISE:** Sit with another person and ask them to tell you about an interesting experience in their life. Practice keeping full eye contact. Ask for clarification and give feedback. Then have the other person ask questions about what they have told you.

74) Pro & Con List

Making a decision is sometimes difficult when I'm not really sure "what is the healthy thing to do." A good way to see the "bigger picture" is to make a Pro & Con list. Make a separate list for each option you have (two options – two sets of lists).

Option #1		Option #2		Option #3	
Pro	Con	Pro	Con	Pro	Con
1.	1.	1.	1.	1.	1.
2.	2.	2.	2.	2.	2.
3.	3.	3.	3.	3.	3.

etc....

Seeing the benefits and drawbacks of each option helps clarify what's really going on and gives a better understanding what the correct choice should be.

75) Do not "put down" anyone

When you "put" someone down you are disrespecting yourself.

Tools for Developing Staff

76) "Belief List" Our "core beliefs" dictate our behavior. Some of our "core beliefs" are false and self-defeating. These false beliefs need to be examined and changed. (see chapter 9)

EXERCISE:

1. Question, question, question your beliefs and perceptions. Be rigorously honest, asking yourself:

"Is this belief or perception healthy for me or is it unhealthy for me?"

"What behavior does this belief direct me to perform?"

"Does this belief or perception keep me living in the past?"

"What is my expectation from believing or perceiving this way?"

"What effect does this belief or perception have on my present?"

2. Challenge your excuses – excuses are usually just rationalizations and justifications constructed to allow you to avoid responsibility for your behavior.

3. Reflect on what in your past (events) may have caused you to develop this belief or perception.
Ask yourself:

"How did I come to believe or see things this way?"

"In what ways have I behaved because I believe this way?"

"What if I was wrong?"

"How could I have perceived it differently?"

"How may I have behaved had I perceived it differently?"

"What may life have been like had I perceived it differently?"

87

4. Stop judging yourself and others. Your judgments are not reality. Because your thinking is distorted, your judgments are your projected illusion of reality based on erroneous thoughts.

5. Be willing to let go of what you don't understand so you can make room for what you can understand and love. There are more things in this world than are dreamt of in your philosophy.

6. Accept that you are almost never upset for the reasons you think.

7. Stop defending a thought system that has hurt you. Stop trying to justify your negative thoughts by making them true.

8. Identify the "payoff" you get from self-defeating behaviors and attitudes. (Payoff such as self-righteousness, negative attention, substance abuse.)

9. Decide how long you are willing to pay the price of your self-defeating behaviors. (Price such as loneliness, hopelessness, isolation, boredom, and health consequences.)

77) Dealing with Fear

Fear is just and emotion – it is not a defect of character – it alerts us to danger so we can take appropriate action to protect ourselves. Fear activates our "fight or flight" mechanism. When confronted with danger, this fight or flight mechanism causes us to have an almost immediate reaction to fight back or flee from the perceived danger. People in ancient days who did not have this response did not live long enough to have offspring.

But Fear unleashed is crippling, paralyzing. Like a deer in the headlights, Fear unleashed puts us in even more danger by preventing us from thinking rationally or taking action to protect ourselves. When this happens, FEAR itself becomes dangerous and becomes an obsession, feeding on itself as it builds. We become victims of our own "false fears." Fear of the unknown, fear of loss, fear of non-acceptance are just a few of these crippling fears. Most of our fears are unfounded and it's these unfounded fears that spin in our head like a squirrel cage out of control.

A few common False Fears are:

Fear of Failure – can cause us to refuse to attempt those things we want to do. We often find ourselves pouring our energy into avoiding failure rather than succeeding at the task at hand. It paralyzes us into non-action.

Fear of Rejection – causes us to keep others at arm's length, thereby not giving them the opportunity to reject us. We often become overly aggressive in a relationship and tend to "people please." This sabotages intimacy and creates in others the exact thing which we fear – rejection.

Fear of being Alone – often causes us to remain in unhealthy or abusive relationships.

Fear of Loss of Self-image – puts us always on guard.

Fear of Powerlessness over others creates within us a desire to control the lives of others.

"Freedom from Fear" doesn't mean having no fear – it means having a life that is not **"dominated by Fear."**

Willingness to share gives us strength in knowing we are not the only ones with these fears and others have gotten through it. Sharing gives us encouragement that we too can get through it. By addressing our fears individually, we begin to develop courage and confidence and begin to see that the "fear itself" was worse than what we feared.

A regular practice of prayer and meditation develops faith that we have help to conquer our fears. To develop faith empowers us to understand that we are never alone, and no matter what happens, we will survive, learn from it, and continue to grow.

EXERCISE:
Ask yourself:

- What exactly is it that I fear?

- What, in reality, is the likelihood this will happen?

- If this does happen, what is the absolute worse outcome?

- Would I be able to continue living if this really did happen?

- What rational steps can I take to protect myself?

- Then take the steps.

- Once your footwork is done, turn it over to your Higher Power.

78) Dealing with Envy

Envious people feel miserable when someone else has something they want. They see other's success as a sign of their own failure and want to attack or destroy what's good in others. If they can't have it – they long for the other person to suffer or loose it.

EXERCISE:
When we find ourselves filled with envy, we need to stop, get honest, and ask ourselves:

1) What do I want to destroy that belongs to somebody else?

2) Why do I feel this way? What is the motivation behind this envy? Do I feel "less than" just because they have it and I don't? Why does that person's possession, accomplishment, or success define me?
3) Is this really my issue and not his?

4) Did this person get or do this just to hurt me?

5) If I had what he has would I want him to feel this way?

6) If yes, then, "Why?"

79) Dealing with Jealousy

Jealous people believe others want to take what is theirs. They view what is theirs as possessions – even people. Possessions are objects to be used and people are not objects. People are to loved. Jealous people confuse love with ownership. They believe that others want to take away something or someone that belongs to them. Incapable of true intimacy, jealous people become paranoid, feeling an intense sense of betrayal and desperation. They end up accusing the very person they feel belongs to them because on some deeper level they believe they are not worthy of the person's love, loyalty, attention, or affection.

EXERCISE:
When we find ourselves jealous, we must stop, get honest, and ask ourselves:

> 1) Do I believe I own this person?
>
> 2) Has this person really done something to warrant me being jealous or is this my own fear of inadequacy?
>
> 3) If this person really has been unfaithful or has betrayed me, then why do I want this person in my life?
>
> (Remember, if I **allow** someone to abuse me – I am guilty of self-abuse)
>
> 4) How is my jealousy hurting me – hurting them?

80) Dealing with Resentment

First, we must understand what resentments are:

- holding onto past hurts and pain – bleeding from old wounds

- reliving past hurts and pain

- obsessing on misery and suffering

- victimizing ourselves again and again by recalling the resentment
- pain which grows more intense each time we recall the resentment
- pain which grows into anger
- anger which grows into hatred
- playing judge, jury, and "would be" executioner
- laying in wait for the time we may get even
- a false sense of protection
- like taking poison and expecting the other person to die
- self abuse
- a prison of our own making
- living in fear, anger, and shame (and living in fear, anger, and shame is **not** living)
- living in weakness (and living is weakness is **not** living)

Once we understand the power and the pain resentment holds over our lives, we must become willing to rid ourselves of resentment. We do this by practicing Tool #82 "Practice the Principle of Forgiveness."

EXERCISE:

1. Write a list of the people you hold resentment toward and the action which caused the resentment.

2. Write down the pain (feelings, emotions) you experience when you recall each resentment.

3. List the angry thoughts you have toward each person.

4. List the things you have done or are doing in the name of hate (avoiding them, gossiping, fantasizing on how to hurt them, keying their car, obsessing on their evil deed, etc.)

5. Now ask yourself, "Am I getting pleasure from my resentment and hate?"

6. Now ask yourself, "Am I keeping this person an enemy so I can blame someone else for my misery?"

7. Now ask yourself, "Am I hanging onto this resentment to have an excuse to be violent, abusive, or angry?"

8. Now ask yourself, "Am I afraid to let go of this pain?"

9. List how your anger and hatreds are hurting you. What's happened to you because of your resentments?

10. Write down why you need to forgive them – how forgiving them will help you.

11. Write two or three good things about each person. (This makes them human again instead of a monster)

12. What would life for you be like if you didn't have this misery to obsess about any longer?

13. Are you willing to stop doing nasty things to this person?

14. Can you pray for this person to receive the good things you want in life?

15. What resentments do you hold toward yourself?

16. Start over with #1 and repeat the process concerning self-resentments.

81) Dealing with Anger

Anger causes a lot of pain in our lives. We often blame our anger for making us say and do things we would never think of doing otherwise. Because of this, anger often gets a "bad wrap." Anger is a normal part of life – an emotion. Emotions are neither good nor bad – they are normal. It's what we do with our emotions – in this case, our Anger – which can be either constructive or destructive. Anger is a gift, a natural and necessary part of life, but it often isn't easy to handle.

People who are emotionally healthy do not hide from their Anger; they use it in a healthy way. Anger alerts you when there is something wrong in your life, it tells you when you've been violated, it tells you to look for the problem, and it tells you to do something to make the situation better.

Healthy Anger is expressed in a way to solve problems – not hurt people. It is good to feel the feeling but chose the behavior. There is no loss of control with healthy Anger because it is expressed in clear ways that others can understand, is temporary, and is let go once an issue is resolved.

Anger is healthy when you:

- **Recognize it: take a time out to –**

   Identify your anger. Honestly ask yourself **why** you are angry.

   Understand your anger is a signal that there is a problem that needs to be addressed.

   Realize it as a normal part of life.

   What are the underlying feelings, the motivation behind, which are driving your anger? – (fear, shame, jealousy, envy, feeling deprived, violated, discounted, rejected, etc.)

   Take **ownership of** and **responsibility for** your anger ("This is what **I** feel and only **I** am responsible for it.")

Tools for Developing Staff

- **Take action: Respond – Don't React!**

  Carefully think through the situation.

  Identify the problem – what needs to be corrected?

  Identify the solution – what steps must be taken to solve the problem?

  Choose the behavior – what is the healthy way to do what is needed without hurting anyone?

  Get proactive – do the footwork that is needed.

  State your anger clearly and calmly in an assertive manner so that others can understand and respond.

  Express you anger in moderation without loosing control.

- **Let it go: Give away the Pain**

  Accept that people are not perfect and suffer from their own issues; they make mistakes, and have to live with themselves.

  Recognize that harboring anger, resentment, and malicious tendencies only hurt you.

  Have you never committed a similar offense?

  Forgive the aggressor.

EXERCISE: (on a separate piece of paper)

1. Think about when you got angry. Explain the circumstance.

2. Did you take a moment to identify your anger – to ask yourself why you were angry?

3. Did you ask yourself what your underlying feelings were – your motivation for being angry?

4. Did you "own" your feelings – take responsibility for them?

5. Did you carefully think through the situation – identify the problem?

6. Did you choose a healthy solution to solve the problem?

7. Did you express your anger in moderation – without losing control?

8. Did you accept that people are not perfect and suffer from their own issues?

9. Did you recognize that harboring resentment and malicious tendencies only hurt you?

10. When you got angry, what did you say?

11. When you got angry, what did you think?

12. When you got angry, what did you do?

13. Did you recognize that you had made a "choice" to get angry?

14. How did the situation end – what was the outcome?

15. What could you have done to change the outcome?

16. How would you handle the same situation if it happened today?

82) Practice the Principle of Forgiveness

Forgiveness releases us from pain, malice, resentment, and hate. In other words, forgiveness frees us from the bondage of retribution. It allows us to climb out of victimhood and take responsibility for our lives, and thus, affect our destiny.

Forgiveness allows us to heal from pain, whether real or imagined, intentional or unintentional – pain which is inflicted by others and even ourselves. Pain distorts and defines our daily lives, our happiness, and our perspective of the world around us. When we refuse to forgive, we shackle ourselves to an expectation of causing pain to others (because I hurt, I want others to hurt). And because we want others to hurt as we have hurt, we defile our dignity and hurt even more.

Forgiveness sets us free to live our lives, celebrating each and every moment. Without forgiveness, we exist in the past, reliving the pain, or we exist in the future, anticipating payback. The reality is that existing in the past or existing in the future is not living. All any of us really have is now. The past is gone and dead. The future is not promised to anyone, young and old alike.

It's important that we understand that forgiveness doesn't protect us from future hurt, it does not mean we forget (we don't want to forget), and doesn't mean that the offending party is not responsible for making reparations for the hurt they've caused. All forgiveness means is that we are no longer going to waste one more precious moment in our life focused on another.

EXERCISE: (on a separate piece of paper)

1. Describe an instance when you were wronged.

2. Describe the feeling this incident caused within you.

3. Own your wound – separate it from others. This is your wound – your pain – it is real.

4. Identify what the injurer did. Identify your actions – what you did. Separate your actions from those of the injurer. You are

responsible for your actions and the injurer is responsible for his actions. Don't take responsibility for what is not yours.

5. Make a conscious choice to become "willing" to relinquish your right to get even. Drop any claims you have against this person.

6. Give up the pain you've been holding onto and stop waiting for it to be resolved. Stop waiting for payback.

83) Setting Vision (chapter 14)

As a manager, you must have a true long-term vision and be passionate about it while, at the same time, you are living in reality. This is what keeps you sane. Part of the "art" of managing from the heart is surrounding yourself with people who also have vision.

As manager I must manage to the "vision." This means that a manager manages in the void between "now" and "vision." As discussed in chapter 7, I must set my vision and then back up to today (my now). This will give me the progression of steps needed to fulfill my vision.

My purpose as manager is the success of both the business and my staff.

Purpose + Vision + Goals + Initiative = Success

Purpose: the inherent value of being; motivation; the intrinsic meaning of one's existence.

Vision: the ability to perceive possibilities.

<u>Goal</u>: a desired state of affairs of a person or of a system.

Initiative: introductory series of steps taken to cause a desired result

Success: long term sustainable growth.

When I have set my vision, I then must back up to my "now." I break down the journey to reach my vision into multiple steps. Each "vision step" is a step solely unto itself, but must build upon the previous step. Each of these "vision steps" becomes a goal.

EXERCISE:

1. Ask your employee to write down their "vision" of where they want to be in their career five years from now.

2. Now ask them to "back up to today" and write down the steps needed to reach their vision.

84) Goal Setting   (see chapter 14)

Most people set goals and then "beat themselves up" or feel like a loser when they don't attain them. The truth is that they didn't really set a goal, they set a dream, and as we learned earlier, dreams just don't happen on their own.

For goals to be viable, they need to possess certain attributes.

A Goal must be:

- Attainable
- Measurable
- Realistic
- Perceptible
- Precise
- Desirable

A goal needs to be understood, properly set, appropriate, and implemented.

Rules for setting effective goals:

1. A goal must be written down. The process of writing it down makes it real

2. Write down goals as positive affirmations. Remember in chapter 9 we discussed how negative self-talk keeps our shame spirals in motion? A goal must be desirable, something I want, and not just something that sounds good.

3. In writing a goal down be careful to be clear and precise.
Write each facet of what applies to achieve the goal.
What is it exactly I want to achieve?
Why do I want to achieve this goal?
What good will come from achieving this goal?
When do I want this goal achieved?
What Boulder and Pebbles will I have to deal with in achieving this goal?

Who else is affected, or will be affected, by me achieving this goal?
What action will I need to take to achieve this goal?

The more information I write down, the more real and perceptible it is. The more I can understand it, the more able I am to visualize and believe it really happening. The more perceptible I make my goal, the more positive my self-talk will become.

4. Once I've written down my goals, I now must evaluate if it is attainable, measurable, and realistic.

5. With my goal laid out on paper, I now need to evaluate if it contradicts any of my other goals. I don't want to be working against myself, setting up roadblocks that get in my own way.

6. At this step, I need to assess whether or not my goal is high enough. I don't want to shortchange myself. It may be attainable. It may be measurable. It may even be realistic, desirable, perceptible, and precise, but is it "settling for something lesser?" Is it limiting?

The more focused I am on my goals, the more successful I will be. If I review my goals daily, visualize myself achieving them, and ask myself if what I am doing now is on track with my goals, I develop positive self-talk and healthy self-esteem (which as we learned in chapter 9 becomes a self-fulfilling prophecy).

EXERCISE: Write down a goal of yours.
  Now:

1. Write each step necessary to achieve this goal.

2. What is it exactly that you want to achieve?

3. Why do you want to achieve this goal?

4. What good will come from achieving this goal?

5. When do I want this goal achieved?

6. What problems will I have to deal with while achieving this goal?

7. Who will be affected and how will they be affected by me achieving this goal?

85) Look at the overall picture

Many times a person will allow some small upsetting detail in a friendship to spoil the whole affair. It is more appropriate to ask yourself: "How important is this to the overall picture of my relationship with the person or persons involved?" This attitude will allow you to have a broader view of the situation. When looked at from a broader viewpoint, you will often discover that the incident is not very important, either to the overall picture, or actually, in itself,. And very seldom is it important enough to justify severing the relationship.

86) Defining "Success Factor"

"Success Factor" pertains to the elements involved in a process which are critical in achieving a goal. In any process, there are a number of steps necessary to align a goal (see chapter 14), keep it on track, evaluate the goal, and see it through to fruition. Some steps are compulsory, some are obligatory, and some are critical.

Critical steps are "Success Factors." These are steps that are essential and must be present if a goal is to be achieved. They cannot be forgotten, set aside, or manipulated. Without these steps, success cannot happen.

EXERCISE: Identify which steps are critical, which are obligatory, and which are compulsory.
If my goal is to drive my car, I must have:

my car

keys

gasoline

wheels

properly inflated tires

automobile insurance

Although compulsory and obligatory steps do enhance the quality and effectivity of my goal, they are not critical in achieving my goal. As manager, I value and attend to all steps. If my goal is worthwhile, I want to achieve it with the highest quality possible. But I want to pinpoint, and pay particular attention to, the critical. Because, if I miss a critical step there is absolutely no chance of success.

One such "success factor" in a person's professional life is "Career Mindedness."

87) Developing Career Mindedness

One of the key factors in instilling Passion in an employee is instructing them in understanding the difference between job and career. As chapter 6 explains, job-minded people "serve time" whereas career-minded people "live time." Career-minded people come to work because they want to; job-minded people because they have to. If I educate my employees on the benefits of being career minded, they become self-motivating, they want to learn and they want to excel.

Job-Minded people view their position and each assignment as just another task to get done before they can go on to something they like.

Career-Minded people understand that each and every thing they do enhances them as a person. Each assignment is a learning opportunity, which increases their talents, experience, knowledge, and abilities.

Taking "ownership" of one's position ignites passion within an individual. Knowing that they are in charge of their lives and their potential is limitless changes life's ball game. A manager from the heart nurtures personal discipline in his employees and integrates the personal benefits of adhering to system standards in this discipline.

Tools for Developing Staff

EXERCISE:

Ask your employee to write a list of ten attributes of their idea of the perfect job. Then ask them to list each in importance of its value. Next, ask them to identify the driving force (the motivation) behind each one.

This exercise helps a person to:

1) identify what is important to them,

2) identify what they value,

3) understand why they find it of value, and

4) possibly reevaluate its importance.

Bottom Line: A "career-minded" employee is self-motivated to learn, participate, and initiate results.

---

88) Set & maintain healthy boundaries, but be flexible enough to change them when it is healthy for **YOU.**   (chapter 12)

By setting and maintaining healthy boundaries, we nurture respect, love, and compassion for ourselves and others. We protect our physical, emotional, psychological, and spiritual being from being violated or abused. Boundaries promote health and growth in those relationships we value most by allowing the other person to participate in the relationship. If others are not aware of our wants and needs, they are not given the choice of fulfilling them.

EXERCISE:

1. Write down three different individuals and something they do that makes you feel uncomfortable, angry, frustrated, hurt, etc.

2. Have you ever told these individuals how their behavior makes you feel?

3. If you have told them and they continue this behavior, why are you still in the relationship?

4. Ask yourself, "Why do I allow someone to treat me like this?"

5. Are you willing to set a proper healthy boundary with this person?

6. Next time you see this person, try the following steps:

a) Validate the other person. Tell them you value them and you value the relationship.

b) Now tell them: **AND** that is why you need to let them know when they do ___(behavior)___ you feel

___(feeling)___ . (Important! make sure you use the word "and" and not "but." "But erases every thing in front of it. "And" enhances everything in front of it.)

c) Now tell them that you would appreciate it if they would refrain from that behavior when they are around you. Don't judge them or their behavior. Just let them know how it makes you feel and you request they refrain from it around you.

d) Now let them know the consequence (what you will or will not do) if they continue.

7. Now the other person has the opportunity to participate in the relationship. They make chose to respect your boundary and the relationship will be nurtured. Or they may choose to disrespect your boundary, in which case you will need to follow through and you will be nurtured.

89) Setting and Maintaining Standards

Standard: a level of quality or excellence with which to judge effectivity.

Effectivity: "Are we doing the right things?"

- **Business Standards**
- **Emotional Standards**

Tools for Developing Staff
- **Moral Standards**

Setting and maintaining standards is a "success factor" (chapter 6) in achieving long-term sustainable growth. This means that without setting and maintaining standards there will be no success – no long-term sustainable growth. Whether in my personal or professional life, standards provide a premise with which to evaluate effectiveness in pursuit of my goals. They compel me to stay on track and remain focused. In effect, standards force me to either "buy in" or "cash out."

In conveying standards, I need to be clear and precise. I need to "spell them out" and then ask for feedback. Asking for feedback allows me to recognize if a person has correctly interpreted my meaning. I must pay close attention to body language, tone of voice, choice of words, etc. I must be understanding and compassionate, and at the same time I must be firm.

There must be a balance between heart and standards. Too much "warm and fuzzy" and I appear sloppy – I undermine the importance of standards. Too much firm and there's no heart – I show no appreciation for the individual.

I inform the individual that it's ultimately their choice (chapter 4) to adhere to the standards or not. I will not make them adhere. I will remind them of the standards if I notice them wavering. But if they choose not to follow standards then Open Heaven is not a place for them, and I will sincerely wish them well in whatever job they choose to go to next.

Deciding whether or not the employee is worth investing time, energy, and effort in is often a fine line.

This can best be determined through:

(1) Measuring performance: one needs to "inspect what they expect."

(2) Holding counseling sessions

(3) Setting goals

(4) Training Sessions

105

(5) Role playing

At the end of each meeting, sign the employee off on the above. And then follow it up with an email to the individual. This validates their participation and documents my intervention. Then, if there is not a quick and continuous movement towards the required standards, a decision must be made to let the employee go.

In "Open Heaven," there are three basic categories of Standards:

> Business Standards
> Emotional Standards
> Moral Standards

EXERCISE: Form groups of three or four and come up with three Standards for each category. Be prepared to explain why you chose them.

---

90) Putting together a staff that has "ownership"

Of their Position:

When an individual has ownership of his or her position, they remain vigilant in their concern of the health of the business. They remain aware and interactive in monitoring the "pulse" of the business. They are quick to alert others of problems and are creative in problem-solving suggestions. In short, they become proactive and have a vested interest in the success of the business.

As manager, I must instill "ownership" in each and every one of my employees. By letting them know how important their position is and how the entire department's level of success is influenced by their effectivity; I validate their importance and the need they serve for the rest of the department.

In order to nurture them in keeping ownership, I must include them in all decisions concerning their position. I must also solicit input on all other areas that influence their position. I find it easier to be respectful of their position as being theirs if I equate it with say – their "violin." If I wanted to do something with their "violin" or change it or use it, I would first ask for their input and then for permission.

By giving an employee "ownership" of his or her position, each becomes an indispensable component of Process.

Of the "Business Plan:"

Acquiring ownership of the Business Plan necessitates the individual participating in the development of the plan. Getting and giving input, being open to feedback, agreeing on goals and setting vision, inspires responsibility and accountability. It's much more difficult to find fault and blame with my own plan than it is with another's.

When I take responsibility for creating something it becomes, at least partly, mine. I am more inclined to respect it, nurture it, take pride in it, and diligently pursue its completion. When I find fault or problems, I am more inclined to be creative and cooperative with those I need help from.

I have an annual "Business Plan" meeting in which we dissect the plan of the previous year and critique what worked and what didn't. Then I let staff create the plan for the upcoming year themselves. Basically, I only facilitate to make sure everyone is heard and considered. If the vision appears to settle (if it appears goals and standards are being set too low) I make suggestions and ask questions based on the pervious year's performance, in a way which implies they may be short changing themselves. If it appears goals and standards are being set too high, I make suggestions and ask questions that lead them to consider more realistic expectations.

Bottom Line: Staff creates the plan they are going to work and live by for the next year – it's their plan – they own it and they must take responsibility for it.

---

91) Paying and Accepting Compliments.

The shortest distance between two people is a smile. Compliment at least five people each day, but be honest (don't just make something up). We often notice things we like about people but neglect to say anything about them. Let people know if their earrings are pretty or you like their smile or their laugh or the way they make you feel.

Practice accepting compliments graciously. Value and respect their opinion. Say "Thank you" when someone pays you a compliment – not "Thank you, but..." When you say "But," you are discounting them, degrading yourself, and feeding your negative self-talk.

92) Starting Your Day Over

Only you can make yourself have a bad day. You can't make me happy, sad, or mad – only I can do that. You might do something which causes me to react a certain way – but how I react is **My Choice**. I will no longer give you my power. I can choose to start my day over at any moment and as often as I want.

93) Be the Person You Want to Become

If you want to become an honest person, be honest today.

If you want to become a compassionate person, be compassionate today.

If you want to become a responsible person, be responsible today.

Just make an effort **today** (do not concern yourself with yesterday or tomorrow) to be the best person you can be. You will find that, day by day, you are becoming that person and then one day you will find that you are that person.

94) Give them the power

Most people shy away from responsibility and often need help in assuming responsibility. As manager, this is where I come in. If I make it their choice it then becomes their responsibility and they are forced to live with the outcome. They must decide themselves what they will do and how they will behave. They begin to evaluate options and weigh effects. In effect, I give them power over their lives.

Most people already know what they should do in any given situation. Most people either don't trust their own decision making and are looking for validation or are looking for someone else to "share the blame" if their plan fails. If I validate their decision then it becomes no longer "their" decision, but becomes "our" decision. If their decision is a success, it's not "their" success it's "our" success. If their decision is not a success, it's now not "their" decision – but my fault.

EXERCISE:

When an employee requests help in making a decision, do exactly that – help him or her make the decision. Be careful not to make it for them.

1) ask them what they think,

2) ask them what options they have considered,

3) suggest other possible options for them to consider,

4) ask if they have weighed the possible outcomes of each option,

5) ask them what effect each option would have on them and on the department,

6) and then I ask them what they chose to do.

By doing this, they learn how to make decisions on their own, and also develop confidence in their decision-making ability. They learn to solve their own problems, celebrate their own triumphs, and learn from their own mistakes (remember, failure isn't failure if you learn a lesson from it). This inspires diligence in an employee to explore solutions to problems and initiate action without running to me to get my "OK" on every little issue.

95) Red Flags for Identifying Burnout:

- Fatigue is the number one red flag in identifying burnout early on. Since most superstars naturally run at a faster pace than others anyway, they often don't recognize fatigue or they explain it away.

- Increased sensitivity to criticism. The individual will begin to take comments seriously he/she would previously have interpreted as just joking around.

- The individual becomes indecisive. Exhaustion, especially coupled with poor nutrition, deprives the brain of needed fuel and rest. The brain loses its ability to function properly, causing the individual to second guess.

- Begins to forget things and has difficulty concentrating. It's difficult to focus on the task at hand when your mind is spinning to make sure you don't miss or forget something. This causes the individual to get further behind, causing even more frustration.

- Becomes frustrated easily, creating more forgetfulness, more difficulty concentrating, and more stress.

- Becomes anti-social and will tend to isolate. Doesn't have time to waste talking to people and will rush people when the individual has to interact.

- Begins to have difficulty getting daily duties completed. Without the ability to concentrate, the individual remembers things he forgot to do later on, compelling the individual to backtrack and correct the error.

- Increase in absenteeism, causing individual to get even further behind.

- Becomes indifferent, developing a "F___ it" attitude.

96) Avoiding Burnout

- Prioritize your workload (see "Time Management Skills" – chapter 14).

- Limit your work hours. Workaholism is an addiction no different from any other addiction. Are you working too many hours each day, week, or month? Do you actually stop work to take a lunch break or do you nibble or gobble while working? Is your job the focus of your life?

- Identify low-yield work.

- Learn to delegate work to others. Asking and accepting help from others is not only OK, it's a good thing.

- Learn to say, "No." It's OK to turn down work when you already have a full plate. You shouldn't feel guilty when you take care of yourself. You wouldn't ask someone else to do more than they're capable of doing.

- Are you using your support network? Are you asking for help? Are you willing to accept help?

- Recognize the "Jobs from Hell." These are jobs which are one time consuming problem after another. Not all jobs are worth taking. If you must take them, then let it be known up front that you will need help.

- Identify personalities and politics. Office personalities and politics are exhausting and easy to get caught up in. Inform your manager if either is interfering with your focus or goals. Be quick to set boundaries (chapter 12), remember you have the right and the responsibility to protect yourself.

- Avoid exhaustion. Get plenty of rest and exercise. Eat right. Lying in front of the TV and stuffing yourself with junk food until the wee hours of the morning is a sure way to feel like you're running on empty. When you leave the workplace – leave the work – don't take it with you.

- Take regular vacations and days off. Americans are infamous for not taking time off. "All work and no play..."

- Don't take work home. If you're going to take work home, you might as well stay at the office. It's a lot more convenient. Why con yourself into thinking you'll be able to spend time with the family?

- Live life in balance. When with your family, your focus should be on your family; when with your friends, your focus should be on your friends; so on and so on.

97) Clearing Boulders and Pebbles is my main job as mentor. After I instruct each individual on the importance of their position, I tell them how badly I want them to be successful. I then help them understand that I realize the only way for me to be successful is for them to be successful – "I succeed only if you succeed."

Part of helping them be successful is to clear all the boulders and even the pebbles from their path. If they stumble, I stumble. If they scrape their knee, I bleed too. They must know and believe that they can count on me for assistance in fulfilling their vision.

It's my job to look for Boulders and Pebbles that get in their way. This includes anything that slows, hinders, impedes, prevents, blocks, or causes them to stumble in the successful completion of their tasks.

Example:

Boulder – suppliers are not delivering material to the worksite when scheduled, causing deadline delays, idle work crews, and extremely unhappy customers.

Pebble – the office copy machine jams when running on the second tray. When the first tray empties, the machine jams, must be cleared, the first tray filled and reset, and the copy job reprogrammed.

Tools for Developing Staff

It's my job to make these problems "go away" for my employees. I need to be vigilant in observing my workplace, but I also need my employees' help. They need to be comfortable in coming to me with problems and confident that these problems will be attended to immediately. Therefore, it's also important I train them to come to me.

A simple thing like putting up with a poorly functioning copy machine causes unneeded delays, employee stress, and even confrontation. It's amazing what employees will tolerate, won't even mention to management, will grumble about among themselves, and then use as an excuse when behind in their work.

In clearing Boulders and Pebbles, I, as mentor, must also "look for the wall" that keeps a person from growing. What's the difference between a two-hundred thousand dollar a year rep and a million dollar a year rep? Simple, only himself.

Often, a sales rep will work and work and grow to a level they never before saw themselves at, and then they plateau. They no sooner leap over one barrier before they set up another.

They accept their new height as the limit and settle. This new limit after awhile then becomes their new mediocrity.

EXERCISE:
Write three Boulders and three Pebbles your office has recently experienced, what effect they've had on your workplace, and what might be done to make them "go away."

98) Identifying Attitudes that lead to Mediocrity

As Instructor, it's my desire to educate my staff on self-defeating behaviors, thinking, and attitudes, which can lead to an employee "shooting himself, or herself, in the foot. I must also be vigilant in monitoring my people daily and catch problems before they become crisis.

The following attitudes lead to mediocrity. These attitudes can filter into a person's life unnoticed, creating dissatisfaction, discouragement, and even despair. These attitudes cause what could be a million-dollar salesman settle for being a two-hundred-thousand-dollar salesman.

Overconfidence about my ability to meet standards without applying myself leads me to believe success will happen by itself. I become lax and pay less attention to detail, and most of all, people.

Impatience concerning my progress causes me to skip or "gloss over" crucial steps, which set the foundation for where I want to go.

Defiance of authority prevents me from being "teachable." Willingness to follow direction is critical to growth. If I am defensive or determined to do things only the way I want to do them, I deprive myself of new experiences which may be more effective.

Isolation from others is dangerous for all human beings. Some of us have problems relating to others.

Complacency is taking life, blessings, miracles, others, me, and even God for granted. When things are going well, I come to expect that happiness, success, love, and joy will just always be there, and I forget all the work it took to get them.

Boredom is a state of self-centeredness. I cannot be bored if I am even a little interested in what is going on around me. The dangerous thing about boredom is that when I am experiencing it, boredom, itself, sucks all motivation out of me to do something about it. Boredom leads to negative thinking.

Negative thinking leads me into a deep sense of futility. I begin to notice all the negative things this world has to offer and fewer, and fewer of the positive. I develop a dangerous, "what's the use, anyway," attitude. I need to "get out of self" very quickly because negative thinking fosters negative self-talk and becomes a descending spiral.

Negative Self-talk is labeling myself as some kind of mistake – deficient as a human being. This keeps my shame spirals in operation.

Tools for Developing Staff

Beating myself up over mistakes and the past keeps me in victimhood. "I deserve to be punished for what I've done, and if you aren't going to punish me – I'll punish myself."

Self Pity / Martyrdom is living in victimhood. Victims become comfortable living in misery, receiving attention and concern from others. I learn to blame others for my pain, but refuse to give it up. By being a victim, I avoid taking responsibility for the problems in my life and feel deserving of sympathy.

Hostility, rage and resentments that are left unresolved will quickly shatter my ability to communicate or be intimate. I will be so uptight and tense that I will repel others (remember the orange). I need to resolve my anger in a healthy way before it explodes into hostility and rage.

Exhaustion, getting "burned-out" occurs when I am over-extending myself, trying to do too much or not eating and sleeping well.

Self-centeredness. There are other people in this world. If I am considerate of them, they return it and more. I get to feel good about me. On the other hand, if I'm not considerate of others, they will surely not be considerate of me. If I'm not getting along with other people, I need to look at myself instead of them. I need to treat people with respect, they deserve it, and so do I.

Pride cripples many of us. Pride, or ego, prevents me from being humble – from surrendering – from accepting life on life's terms. It prevents me from admitting a mistake or asking for help. I become defensive and closed off. Pride keeps me from being totally honest with myself and in my dealings with others (which in turn prevents me from the most wondrous discovery of all – me).

As Instructor, I first need to make my staff aware of what these attitudes are, how they work, and the affect they have on the individual and the department in general. This often enables

115

a staff member to recognize one of these attitudes in themselves and make corrections as they occur.

This level of self-awareness allows an individual to self-monitor and prevent spiraling. As they become more adept at this process, the process itself becomes easier, quicker, and eventually, second nature – automatic.

Bottom Line: Self-monitoring employees are more efficient, produce more, have less downtime, and require no stress leave.

---

99) Freedom of Responsibility

As Instructor, I must also tutor my employees on the power and freedom that come from the taking and giving of responsibility for the choices they make. They must learn that all they really have power over are the choices they make, and all they really have control over is their attitude.

When an employee accepts responsibility (chapter 9) for the choices he or she makes, we can get down to taking care of business. We don't waste time arguing or debating who did what or didn't do what. We can identify and understand the problem, find a solution, and become proactive.

- Identify the problem.

- Understand the problem.

- Find a solution:
  What worked? Why did it work?
  What didn't work? Why didn't it work?

- How can we change what didn't work to make it work?

- Get proactive.

Usually, employees don't want to accept responsibility out of fear of penalty; disfavor, embarrassment, loss of position or standing, etc. But in Open Heaven, staff knows that the manager realizes mistakes will be made from time-to-time and won't judge the individual, but instead, is willing to assist them. This allows the individual to focus on problem solving, not "ass saving."

Bottom Line: This saves time, energy, effort, and productivity.

Made in the
USA
Columbia, SC